Active Learning:
Creating Excitement in the Classr

by Charles C. Bonwell and James A. Eis(

ASHE-ERIC Higher Education Report No. 1, 1991

Prepared by

Clearinghouse on Higher Education
The George Washington University

In cooperation with

Association for the Study
of Higher Education

Published by

School of Education and Human Development
The George Washington University

Jonathan D. Fife, Series Editor

Cite as
Bonwell, Charles C., and James A. Eison. 1991. *Active Learn-
ing: Creating Excitement in the Classroom.* ASHE-ERIC Higher
Education Report No. 1. Washington, D.C.: The George
Washington University, School of Education and Human
Development.

Library of Congress Catalog Card Number 91-65608
ISSN 0884-0040
ISBN 1-878380-08-7

Managing Editor: Bryan Hollister
Manuscript Editor: Barbara Fishel, Editech
Cover design by Michael David Brown, Rockville, Maryland

The ERIC Clearinghouse on Higher Education invites individuals to submit proposals for writing monographs for the
ASHE-ERIC Higher Education Report series. Proposals must
include:
1. A detailed manuscript proposal of not more than five pages.
2. A chapter-by-chapter outline.
3. A 75-word summary to be used by several review committees for the initial screening and rating of each proposal.
4. A vita and a writing sample.

ERIC **Clearinghouse on Higher Education**
School of Education and Human Development
The George Washington University
One Dupont Circle, Suite 630
Washington, DC 20036-1183

This publication was prepared partially with funding from
the Office of Educational Research and Improvement, U.S.
Department of Education, under contract no. ED RI-88-062014.
The opinions expressed in this report do not necessarily
reflect the positions or policies of OERI or the Department.

EXECUTIVE SUMMARY

Throughout the 1980s, numerous leaders in the field of higher education (Cross 1987) and a series of national reports (Study Group 1984) repeatedly urged college and university faculty to actively involve and engage students in the process of learning. Despite the urgency of these calls, research consistently has shown that traditional lecture methods, in which professors talk and students listen, dominate college and university classrooms. It is therefore important to know the nature of active learning, the empirical research on its use, the common obstacles and barriers that give rise to faculty members' resistance to interactive instructional techniques, and how faculty, faculty developers, administrators, and educational researchers can make real the promise of active learning.

What Is Active Learning and Why Is It Important?

Surprisingly, educators' use of the term "active learning" has relied more on intuitive understanding than a common definition. Consequently, many faculty assert that all learning is inherently active and that students are therefore actively involved while listening to formal presentations in the classroom. Analysis of the research literature (Chickering and Gamson 1987), however, suggests that students must do more than just listen: They must read, write, discuss, or be engaged in solving problems. Most important, to be actively involved, students must engage in such higher-order thinking tasks as analysis, synthesis, and evaluation. Within this context, it is proposed that strategies promoting active learning be defined as instructional activities involving students in doing things and thinking about what they are doing.

Use of these techniques in the classroom is vital because of their powerful impact upon students' learning. For example, several studies have shown that students prefer strategies promoting active learning to traditional lectures. Other research studies evaluating students' achievement have demonstrated that many strategies promoting active learning are comparable to lectures in promoting the mastery of content but superior to lectures in promoting the development of students' skills in thinking and writing. Further, some cognitive research has shown that a significant number of individuals have learning styles best served by pedagogical techniques other than lecturing. Therefore, a thoughtful and scholarly approach to skillful teaching requires that faculty become knowledgeable about the many ways strategies promoting active learning have been successfully used across the disciplines. Further, each faculty member should engage in self-reflection, exploring his or her personal willingness to experiment with alternative approaches to instruction.

How Can Active Learning Be Incorporated In the Classroom?

The modification of traditional lectures (Penner 1984) is one way to incorporate active learning in the classroom. Research has demonstrated, for example, that if a faculty member allows students to consolidate their notes by pausing three times for two minutes each during a lecture, students will learn significantly more information (Ruhl, Hughes, and Schloss 1987). Two other simple yet effective ways to involve students during a lecture are to insert brief demonstrations or short, ungraded writing exercises followed by class discussion. Certain alternatives to the lecture format further increase students' level of engagement: (1) the feedback lecture, which consists of two minilectures separated by a small-group study session built around a study guide, and (2) the guided lecture, in which students listen to a 20- to 30-minute presentation without taking notes, followed by their writing for five minutes what they remember and spending the remainder of the class period in small groups clarifying and elaborating the material.

These approaches to modifying traditional lectures give rise to a common question: "Is the large class a special case?" Although a commonly shared perception among faculty is that large classes preclude significant participation by students, the literature suggests otherwise (Frederick 1986). For example, a faculty member in a class of any size can instruct students to write a brief response to a question, to pair with a partner seated on the left or right, and then to compare and contrast both responses.

Discussion in class is one of the most common strategies promoting active learning—with good reason. If the objectives of a course are to promote long-term retention of information, to motivate students toward further learning, to allow students to apply information in new settings, or to develop students' thinking skills, then discussion is preferable to lecture (McKeachie et al. 1986). Research has suggested, however, that to achieve these goals faculty must be knowledgeable of alternative techniques and strategies for questioning and discussion (Hyman 1980) and must create a supportive intellectual and emotional environment that encourages students to take risks (Lowman 1984).

Several additional strategies promoting active learning have been similarly shown to influence favorably students' attitudes and achievement. Visual-based instruction, for example, can provide a helpful focal point for other interactive techniques. In-class writing across the disciplines is another productive way to involve students in doing things and thinking about the things they are doing. Two popular instructional strategies based on problem-solving models include the case study method of instruction and Guided Design. Other active learning pedagogies worthy of instructors' use include cooperative learning, debates, drama, role playing and simulation, and peer teaching. In short, the published literature on alternatives to traditional classroom presentations provides a rich menu of different approaches faculty can readily add to their repertoire of instructional skills.

What Are the Barriers?

To address adequately why most faculty have not embraced recent calls for educational reform, it is necessary first to identify and understand common barriers to instructional change, including:

- The powerful influence of educational tradition;
- Faculty self-perceptions and self-definition of roles;
- The discomfort and anxiety that change creates;
- The limited incentives for faculty to change.

But certain specific obstacles are associated with the use of active learning:

- The difficulty in adequately covering the assigned course content in the limited class time available;
- A possible increase in the amount of preparation time;
- The difficulty of using active learning in large classes;
- A lack of needed materials, equipment, or resources.

Perhaps the single greatest barrier of all, however, is the fact that faculty members' efforts to employ active learning involve risk—the risks that students will not participate, use higher-order thinking, or learn sufficient content, that faculty members will feel a loss of control, lack necessary skills, or be criticized for teaching in unorthodox ways. Each obstacle or barrier and type of risk, however, can be successfully overcome through careful, thoughtful planning.

What Conclusions Should Be Drawn and Recommendations Made?

The reform of instructional practice in higher education must begin with faculty members' efforts. An excellent first step is to select strategies promoting active learning that one can feel comfortable with. Such low-risk strategies are typically of short duration, structured and planned, focused on subject matter that is neither too abstract nor too controversial, and familiar to both the faculty member and the students.

Conversely, greater levels of risk occur when one or more of these dimensions is altered. Faculty can successfully overcome each of the major obstacles or barriers to the use of active learning by gradually incorporating teaching strategies requiring more activity from students and/or greater risk into their regular style of instruction.

Faculty developers can help stimulate and support faculty members' efforts to change by highlighting the instructional importance of active learning in the newsletters and publications they distribute. Further, the use of active learning should become both the subject matter of faculty development workshops and the instructional method used to facilitate such programs. And it is important that faculty developers recognize the need to provide follow-up to, and support for, faculty members' efforts to change.

Academic administrators can help these initiatives by recognizing and rewarding excellent teaching in general and the adoption of instructional innovations in particular. Comprehensive programs to demonstrate this type of administrative commitment (Cochran 1989) should address:

- Institutional employment policies and practices;
- The allocation of adequate resources for instructional development; and
- The development of strategic administrative action plans.

Equally important is the need for more rigorous research to provide a scientific foundation to guide future practices

in the classroom. Currently, most published articles on active
learning have been descriptive accounts rather than empirical
investigations, many are out of date, either chronologically
or methodologically, and a large number of important conceptual issues have never been explored. New qualitative
and quantitative research should:

- Examine strategies that enhance students' learning from
  presentations;
- Explore the impact of previously overlooked, yet edu-
  cationally significant, characteristics of students, such as
  gender, different learning styles, or stage of intellectual
  development;
- Be disseminated in journals widely read by faculty.

In retrospect, it appears that previous classroom initiatives
and written materials about active learning have all too often
been isolated and fragmented. The resulting pedagogical
efforts have therefore lacked coherence, and the goal of interactive classrooms has remained unfulfilled. Through the coordinated efforts of individual faculty, faculty developers, academic administrators, and educational researchers, however,
higher education in the coming decade *can* make real the
promise of active learning!

ADVISORY BOARD

Alberto Calbrera
Arizona State University

Carol Everly Floyd
Board of Regents of the Regency Universities System
State of Illinois

L. Jackson Newell
University of Utah

Barbara Taylor
Association of Governing Boards of Universities and Colleges

J. Fredericks Volkwein
State University of New York–Albany

Bobby Wright
Pennsylvania State University

CONSULTING EDITORS

Brenda M. Albright
State of Tennessee Higher Education Commission

Walter R. Allen
University of California

William E. Becker
Indiana University

Louis W. Bender
Florida State University

Paul T. Brinkman
National Center for Higher Education Management Systems

David G. Brown
University of North Carolina–Asheville

David W. Chapman
State University of New York–Albany

Jay L. Chronister
University of Virginia

Linda Clement
University of Maryland

Richard A. Couto
Tennessee State University

Peter Frederick
Wabash College

Mildred Garcia
Montclair State College

Edward R. Hines
Illinois State University

Don Hossler
Indiana University

John L. Howarth
Private Consultant

William Ihlanfeldt
Northwestern University

Greg Johnson
Harvard College

REVIEW PANEL

Charles Adams
University of Massachusetts–Amherst

Richard Alfred
University of Michigan

Philip G. Altbach
State University of New York–Buffalo

Louis C. Attinasi, Jr.
University of Houston

Ann E. Austin
Vanderbilt University

Robert J. Barak
Iowa State Board of Regents

Alan Bayer
Virginia Polytechnic Institute and State University

John P. Bean
Indiana University

Louis W. Bender
Florida State University

Carol Bland
University of Minnesota

Deane G. Bornheimer
New York University

John A. Centra
Syracuse University

Arthur W. Chickering
George Mason University

Jay L. Chronister
University of Virginia

Mary Jo Clark
San Juan Community College

Shirley M. Clark
Oregon State System of Higher Education

Darrel A. Clowes
Virginia Polytechnic Institute and State University

CONTENTS

Foreword	**xvii**
Acknowledgments	**xix**

What Is Active Learning?	**1**
Defining Active Learning	1
How Much Active Learning Occurs?	2
What Leading Educators Say	3
A Serious Problem for Higher Education	4

The Modified Lecture	**7**
Pausing for Enhanced Retention and Comprehension	10
Tests and Quizzes	11
Demonstrations	12
Alternative Formats for Lectures	13
Student-Generated Questions	14
Are Large Classes a Special Case?	14

Questioning and Discussion	**21**
A Supportive Classroom Environment	21
Discussion Material	23
Types of Questions	24
Effective Techniques of Questioning	27
Discussion Strategies and Style	29

Additional Strategies Promoting Active Learning	**33**
Visual-Based Instruction	33
Writing in Class	35
Problem Solving	38
Computer-Based Instruction	41
Cooperative Learning	43
Debates	45
Drama	46
Role Playing, Simulations, and Games	47
Peer Teaching	50

Barriers to Change in the Classroom	**53**
Global Barriers to Change	53
Barriers to the Use of Active Learning	59
Risk: The Greatest Barrier of All	62

Conclusions and Recommendations	**65**
The Role of College and University Faculty	65
The Role of Faculty Developers	71
The Role of Campus Administrators	73
The Role of Educational Researchers	76

References	**81**
Index	**95**

FOREWORD

Increasingly, college and university faculty are being held accountable for the effectiveness of their teaching. Research has clearly demonstrated that the more college students become involved with the education process, the more they learn. Yet most faculty continue to use one of the most student-passive forms of teaching: the lecture. When educators are asked why they prefer this method, their most frequent response is that they are comfortable with it.

Lecturing is the method many faculty experienced most frequently as students. Some faculty feel that by lecturing, they have greater control over the content and amount of information dispensed. Once having conveyed this information, lecturers feel they have fulfilled their responsibility to impart its meaning to the students. But faced with low effectiveness, both students and academic leaders are becoming less satisfied with this approach to teaching.

The concept of active learning—that is, increasing students' involvement in the learning process—is an indispensable technique for increasing the effectiveness of teaching. In many cases, active learning can be employed without any increased costs and with only a modest change in current teaching practices. It is low risk with high return.

Charles C. Bonwell, director of the Center for Teaching and Learning and a professor in the Department of History at Southeast Missouri State University, and James A. Eison, founding director of the Center for Teaching Enhancement at the University of South Florida, present the elements and advantages of active learning in this report. They discuss modifications to traditional lectures, alternative lecture formats, additional active learning strategies, the roles of researchers and various college and university personnel, and obstacles to the use of active learning.

Teaching is both an art and a learned skill. Faculty who are dissatisfied with their current methods of teaching will find this report very useful as they examine the various options available for improving the impact of their teaching. Academic leaders will also find this report worthwhile as they establish new goals and directions and raise expectations for their faculty.

Jonathan D. Fife
Series Editor, Professor, and
Director, ERIC Clearinghouse on Higher Education

ACKNOWLEDGMENTS

The authors owe a special thanks to Jonathan Fife, editor of the ASHE-ERIC Research Reports, for his perceptive comments and cheerful assistance. Similarly, we would like to thank our faculty, staff, and administrative colleagues at Southeast Missouri State University and the University of South Florida for the stimulation and support they have provided. In addition, workshop participants in sessions led by the authors, who now number several thousand, have helped us refine our thinking about active learning; we thank them all! On a more personal level, we want to acknowledge the countless hours spent by our clerical staff, Lisa Hart, Theresa Burke, and Christy Montgomery, who have typed and proofed numerous versions of this monograph. Last, C.B. wishes to thank his closest friend and most ardent cheerleader, Marcia.

WHAT IS ACTIVE LEARNING?

Active inquiry, not passive absorption, is what engages students. It should pervade the curriculum (Johnson et al. 1989, p. 68).

Defining Active Learning

Despite its frequent appearance in the literature on higher education, the term "active learning" seems to lack an identifiable origin or a common definition. John Dewey, for example, in his classic work, *Democracy and Education,* noted briefly that learning is "something an individual does when he studies. It is an active, personally conducted affair" (1924, p. 390); more recent speakers and authors, however, have typically relied upon an intuitive understanding of the term. Ambiguity and confusion have been the all-too-often result. For example, a national report, *Involvement in Learning,* urges faculty to use active modes of learning more extensively (Study Group 1984). Based on interviews with 89 faculty on various campuses, however, other researchers note that faculty members are not familiar with the meaning of the term "involvement" as currently used in higher education (Stark et al. 1988). For faculty, "involvement appeared to be synonymous with 'listening,' 'paying attention,' or 'being alert' rather than signifying engagement with the material being learned" (p. 95).

Another source of confusion resides in two questions faculty commonly ask: "Can one ever learn in a passive fashion?" and "Doesn't the term 'learning' automatically involve some type of activity?" One response to these questions is found in the observation that:

> *Students learn both passively and actively. Passive learning takes place when students take on the role of "receptacles of knowledge"; that is, they do not directly participate in the learning process. . . . Active learning is more likely to take place when students are doing something besides listening* (Ryan and Martens 1989, p. 20).

It is even more helpful to envision a continuum of possible classroom actions that increase in students' activity. The passive end of the continuum would include such things as sitting in class inattentively, dividing one's concentration between episodes of daydreaming and periods of attentiveness to the lecture, and listening and occasionally taking literal

Greater emphasis is placed on the students' exploration of their own attitudes and values.

notes. Increased activity would include making a sustained effort to take exemplary nonliteral, paraphrased lecture notes, monitoring one's level of understanding the subject matter and writing questions in the lecture notes when confused, and asking questions at appropriate points in an instructor's presentation. Students' involvement can be further increased by the instructor's use of such strategies as using discussion-leading and questioning techniques skillfully to engage students in a personal exploration of the subject matter, having students engage in short writing activities in class followed by sharing what they have written in small groups, and using presentations, debates, and role-playing activities by students. (The subsequent three sections analyze these ways to increase students' active learning more extensively.)

Though the term "active learning" has never been precisely defined in educational literature, some general characteristics are commonly associated with the use of strategies promoting active learning in the classroom:

- Students are involved in more than listening.
- Less emphasis is placed on transmitting information and more on developing students' skills.
- Students are involved in higher-order thinking (analysis, synthesis, evaluation).
- Students are engaged in activities (e.g., reading, discussing, writing).
- Greater emphasis is placed on students' exploration of their own attitudes and values.

To provide a working definition for the following analysis, the authors propose that, given these characteristics and in the context of the college classroom, active learning be defined as anything that "involves students in doing things and thinking about the things they are doing."

How Much Active Learning Occurs?

One important question that must be explored is How much active learning occurs in a typical classroom? Nearly 30 years ago, one answer was that "college teaching and lecturing have been so long associated that when one pictures a college professor in the classroom, he almost inevitably pictures him as lecturing" (McKeachie, cited in Gage 1963, p. 1125). The best available data strongly support the validity of that claim, both then and now. A survey of faculty on 24 campuses, for example, asked them to describe the first undergraduate class they met each week (Blackburn et al. 1980). This technique, while covering a wide assortment of courses, class sizes, and levels of students, avoided bias in selection. Between 73 percent and 83 percent of the faculty reported that their primary method of instruction was lecturing, causing the authors to conclude: "Give a faculty almost any kind of class in any subject, large or small, upper or lower division, and they will lecture" (p. 41). Similarly, the most recent extensive survey of U.S. university professors found lecturing to be the mode of instruction of 89 percent of the physical scientists and mathematicians, 81 percent of the social scientists, and 61 percent of the humanities faculty (although 81 percent of the art historians and 90 percent of the philosophers lectured) (Thielens 1987).

What Leading Educators Say
Numerous researchers and recent national reports have described clearly the need for active learning in the classroom.

Learning is not a spectator sport. Students do not learn much just by sitting in class listening to teachers, memorizing prepackaged assignments, and spitting out answers. They must talk about what they are learning, write about it, relate it to past experiences, apply it to their daily lives. They must make what they learn part of themselves (Chickering and Gamson 1987, p. 3).

Students learn what they care about and remember what they understand (Ericksen 1984, p. 51).

When students are actively involved in . . . learning . . . , they learn more than when they are passive recipients of instruction (Cross 1987, p. 4).

Students learn by becoming involved. . . . Student involvement refers to the amount of physical and psychological energy that the student devotes to the academic experience (Astin 1985, pp. 133–34).

Others have issued similar calls for the use of strategies promoting active learning, including the Association of American

Colleges's Task Group on General Education (1988), the
National Association of Student Personnel Administrators
(1987), and the Study Group on the Conditions of Excellence
in American Higher Education (1984).

A Serious Problem for Higher Education

A description of eight noticeable gaps in the practice of higher
education includes the gap between teaching and learning,
the gap between teaching and testing, and the gap between
educational research and practice (Cross 1988). A serious gap
also exists between how faculty typically teach (i.e., relying
largely on the lecture method) and how they know they
should teach (i.e, employing active learning to facilitate students' mastery of subject matter, develop intellectual skills,
and form personal attitudes and values). Successive sections
explore ways to eliminate this gap by modifying the lecture,
conducting more stimulating class discussions, and using
other approaches to active learning. The text also presents
an analysis of barriers to change in the classroom and offers
conclusions and recommendations for faculty, faculty developers, administrators, and educational researchers.

The development of this monograph has been guided by
several principles:

- Material published since 1980 received primary emphasis.
- Research-based rather than descriptive studies were used
  wherever possible.
- The focus was on studies conducted within higher education, omitting active learning strategies that take place
  only outside the classroom (e.g., field trips, practicums,
  and internships).
- Strategies promoting active learning upon which an entire
  course is structured, such as personalized systems of
  instruction, were similarly not reported.
- The work was designed to provide an extensive review
  of the literature rather than to be an extensive "how-to-
  do-it-better" book, in accordance with ASHE-ERIC
  guidelines.

Two final points should reduce potential confusion among
readers. First, several authors of descriptive studies have
claimed that the particular active learning strategy they
employed was superior to traditional instructional approaches.

Without carefully collected quantitative or qualitative data to support such claims, however, such convictions should carry no more weight then the personal convictions of other faculty who favor traditional instructional approaches. Readers should be similarly advised that whenever the term "significant" is used in *this* text, "significant" refers specifically to a reported statistically significant difference between two or more classes or instructional approaches.

Second, though the use of strategies promoting active learning in *all* college and university classrooms is a commendable objective, various instructional approaches discussed in this text are more appropriate for some disciplines than others. Regardless of a reader's disciplinary background, the authors hope that each one will explore the power of active learning through critical analysis and personal application of the research.

THE MODIFIED LECTURE

When asked why he lectures, one professor responded:

> *It is tradition. It was part of my training, and seems like what I should be doing. I feel somehow guilty when I am not lecturing* (Creed 1986, p. 25).

This candid statement suggests one of the great dilemmas faced by all who teach at the postsecondary level today. Lecturing is virtually synonymous with teaching. It was the dominant method by which we were taught—and it is the method by which most of us teach. When books like this one or faculty development workshops advocate alternative approaches, many faculty members become defensive, and discussions can quickly degenerate into heated debates where sides are clearly—sometimes angrily—drawn. In some instances, overexuberant advocates of active learning have become adversaries of colleagues who use traditional methods, dooming any hope of changing others' teaching methods—no matter how persuasive the evidence that such change should take place! This tension is unfortunate. Such characterizations of "us" and "them" serve little purpose. Better is an alternative approach that recognizes that one's choice of an instructional method is best viewed as appropriate or inappropriate only when placed within a context that considers the professor's specific objectives, the complexity of the subject matter, the physical setting of the classroom, and the capabilities of the learners. The challenge is to choose a suitable method at the appropriate time. Understanding the strengths and weaknesses of the lecture method is a helpful starting point.

Lectures have a number of characteristics that can make them a desirable approach in the classroom. An enthusiastic lecturer can:

1. Communicate the intrinsic interest of the subject matter differently from any other media;
2. Provide students with a thoughtful, scholarly role model to emulate;
3. Describe subject matter that is otherwise unavailable, such as original research or current developments not yet published in traditional textbooks;
4. Organize material in ways to meet the particular needs of a given audience; and
5. Efficiently deliver large amounts of information if certain conditions are met (Chism et al. 1989).

In addition, lectures are cost-effective in that they can reach many listeners at one time, they present a minimum threat to students in that they are not required to actively participate, and they provide an advantage for those students who find learning by listening enjoyable (Chism et al. 1989).

As most students will attest, not all lectures or lecturers achieve these goals. Research findings suggest that a number of identifiable attributes must be implemented to make a lecture truly effective. For instance, students remember material presented at the beginning of a lecture on tests of immediate recall better than information presented in the middle or at the end of the lecture. To some extent, the effectiveness of the lecture varies inversely with the difficulty of the material presented, and listeners retain factual material better when it is presented in short sentences rather than in long sentences. Speaking extemporaneously is more effective than reading from lecture notes, and it is desirable to change the pitch, intensity, and timbre of one's voice (Verner and Dickinson 1967).

These characteristics presume that the lecturer is an enthusiastic and knowledgeable scholar. Anyone familiar with higher education recognizes that most campuses have a few gifted practitioners of the formal 50-minute lecture who routinely achieve this ideal and who regularly provide students with spellbinding motivational experiences. Even if it is assumed that most lecturers possess these necessary characteristics, research suggests that *the exclusive use of the lecture in the classroom constrains students' learning.*

One of the most important problems associated with total reliance on the lecture method is the inability of most individuals to listen effectively to any lecturer, no matter how skillful, over a sustained period. For example, research on the learning experiences of college students exposed to straight lectures found that after an initial settling-in period of five minutes, students readily assimilated material for the next five minutes. Ten to 20 minutes into the lecture, however, confusion and boredom set in and assimilation fell off rapidly, remaining at a low state until a brief period toward the end of the lecture when students were revived by the knowledge that the lecture would soon be over (D.H. Lloyd, cited in Penner 1984). Similarly, the concentration of medical students, a population that presumably is highly motivated, "rose sharply to reach a maximum in 10 [to] 15 minutes and fell steadily thereafter" (Stuart and Rutherford 1978, p. 514). A study of how effectively students concentrated during a 50-minute lecture that analyzed the percentage of content they recorded in their lecture notes at different time intervals through the lecture found that students noted approximately 41 percent of the content presented during the first 15 minutes, 25 percent in a 30-minute period, but only 20 percent during 45 minutes (J. McLeish, cited in Penner 1984).

Research also suggests that the relative effectiveness of a lecture depends on the educational level of the audience. "In general, very little of a lecture can be recalled except in the case of listeners with above-average education and intelligence" (Verner and Dickinson 1967, p. 90). (Given the placement scores of many freshmen, this statement should give pause to most instructors in higher education.) Even with bright, competent people listening to an interesting topic presented by a knowledgeable speaker, several serious problems remain. What college professor has not experienced the following scenario?

Ten percent of the audience displayed signs of inattention within 15 minutes. After 18 minutes one-third of the audience and 10 percent of the platform guests were fidgeting. At 35 minutes everyone was inattentive; at 45 minutes, trance was more noticeable than fidgeting; and at 47 minutes some were asleep and at least one was reading. A casual check 24 hours later revealed that the audience recalled only insignificant details, [which] were generally wrong (Verner and Dickinson 1967, p. 90).

Such studies suggest that lengthy lectures are not conducive to efficient learning—a charge usually leveled at other, less direct methods of teaching.

A related line of research concluded that, with the possible exception of programmed learning, the lecture was *no more effective* in transmitting information than other methods (Bligh 1972). More important, the lecture was clearly *less effective* in promoting thought or in changing attitudes. Similarly, the results of 58 studies from 1928 to 1967 that compared various characteristics of lectures and discussions show that lecturing did not differ significantly from discussions in helping students to acquire facts and principles (Costin 1972). Discussion, however, was superior to lectures in developing students' ability to solve problems. As the emphasis of a course moved from lecture to discussion, more students seemed to approve of the course. The implications of this finding are especially important for instructors of introductory courses where disciplines often attempt to attract future majors.

> *The test of a good teacher . . . is, "Do you regard 'learning' as a noun or a verb?" If as a noun, as a thing to be possessed and passed along, then you present your truths, neatly packaged, to your students. But if you see "learning" as a verb[,] the process is different. The good teacher has learning, but tries to instill in students the desire to learn, and demonstrates the ways one goes about "learning"* (Schorske, cited in McCleery 1986, p. 106).

The evidence suggests that if an instructor's goals are not only to impart information but also to develop cognitive skills and to change attitudes, then alternative teaching strategies should be interwoven with the lecture method during classroom presentations. The following approaches are designed to help instructors achieve that goal.

Pausing for Enhanced Retention and Comprehension
Modifying a lecture to enhance students' learning by pausing at least three times to allow discussions among students puts the focus on clarifying and assimilating the information presented (Rowe 1980), and empirical data support this contention (Ruhl, Hughes, and Schloss 1987). In a follow-up study, an instructor paused for two minutes on three occasions during each of five lectures; the intervals between pauses ranged from 12 to 18 minutes. During the pauses, while students worked in pairs to discuss and rework their notes, no interaction occurred between instructor and students. At the end of each lecture, students were given three minutes to write down everything they could remember from the lecture (free recall); 12 days after the last lecture, the students were also given a 65-item multiple-choice test to measure long-term retention. A control group received the same lectures (using the same anecdotes and visual aids) and was similarly tested. In two separate courses repeated over two semesters, the results were striking and consistent: Students hearing the lectures where the instructor paused did significantly better on

the free-recall quizzes and the comprehensive test. In fact, the magnitude of the difference in mean scores between the two groups was large enough to make a difference of up to two letter grades, depending on cutoff points (Ruhl, Hughes, and Schloss 1987). These results—obtained with minimal effort on the instructor's part and the loss of only six minutes of lecture time per class session—constitute an effective low-risk approach for increasing students' involvement that every instructor could use.

Tests and Quizzes

In the context of the definition of active learning presented in the previous section, short quizzes and tests qualify as a method of active learning. For instance, one way to modify traditional lectures to increase students' learning is to include an immediate mastery test of the subject material covered. Research conducted in the 1920s, often replicated, details students' "forgetting curve" for lecture material, finding that the average student had immediate recall of 62 percent of the information presented but that recall declined to approximately 45 percent after three or four days and fell to only 24 percent after eight weeks. If students were asked to take an examination immediately after the lecture, however, they retained almost twice as much information, both factual and conceptual, after eight weeks (Menges 1988).

These results suggest that short quizzes and hour-long examinations are powerful influences upon, if not the major determinant of, what students study and how students learn (Milton and Eison 1983). In one student's words:

> *When studying for completion, multiple-choice, or true-false examinations, I find that I do not attempt to get a general view of the material—I try to learn the facts or memorize the statements. When I study for an essay examination, I read and reread the material with the object of getting not only the facts but also a general concept of the material* (Meyer 1935, p. 31).

This statement illustrates several important points, perhaps the most significant of which for educators is the fact that scheduling an exam stimulates students to study. Further, the type of exam students anticipate directly influences the focus of their studying. And finally, students have not changed dra-

As the emphasis of a course moved from lecture to discussion, more students seemed to approve of the course.

matically over the last 50 years; this student's observations are still true today.

Paradoxically, despite the considerable national attention currently devoted to the issue of assessing educational outcomes in higher education, most faculty pay little or no attention to the potential impact of tests on students' learning. Two explanations might account for this puzzling situation. First:

> *Examining in higher education is not on the whole looked upon as one of the more interesting aspects of academic life. Examinations in fact are often regarded as unfortunate and even distasteful distractions from teaching and research* (Cox 1967, p. 352).

Though this observation was made initially about British faculty, it accurately portrays the view of many faculty in the United States.

Second, the evaluative purposes of tests (providing for many the primary basis for determining and assigning grades) receive far greater attention than the nonevaluative purposes (Milton, Pollio, and Eison 1986). In the context of strategies promoting active learning used in the classroom, tests provide a rather obvious way to involve students in doing something and getting them to think about what they are doing.

Demonstrations

Demonstrations during a lecture, particularly in the sciences, can be used to stimulate students' curiosity and to improve their understanding of conceptual material and processes, particularly when the demonstration invites students to participate in the investigative process through the use of such questions as "What will happen if we . . .?" Demonstrations can also serve as a vehicle for instructors to share attitudes about the tentative and changing nature of knowledge in their discipline, with a goal of motivating students to engage in experimentation on their own (Shakhashiri 1984). A caveat is necessary, however. One study has clearly shown that students who actively engaged in laboratory experiments designed to illustrate specific principles of physics had less difficulty learning those principles than students who merely saw a similar demonstration illustrating the principle given during a lecture (Okpala and Onocha 1988).

Alternative Formats for Lectures

Six colleagues at Oregon State University developed a structured lecture/discussion approach using Wales's and Stager's (1978) guided design process (Osterman 1984). After examining the advantages and disadvantages of several alternative teaching methods, the group devised what it called the "feedback lecture." Carefully designed, the feedback lecture is built around a supplemental study guide that provides assigned readings, pre- and posttests, learning objectives, and an outline of lecture notes. The basic format of the feedback lecture consists of two minilectures approximately 20 minutes long separated by a small-group study session where students work in pairs responding to a discussion question focused on the lecture material provided by the instructor. An evaluation of the approach over three semesters showed students ($N = 273$) to rate the system very positively. Ninety-nine percent of the students questioned stated that they found the discussion break to be either "useful" or "extremely useful." Students' motivation would seem to be reflected in the responses to the question, "Did you answer the pretest and posttest included in the study guide?" Ninety-three percent stated that they did so "often" or "always." Finally, 88 percent of the students responded that they would prefer a course taught using the feedback lecture to a straight lecture course if offered the choice. The unstated disadvantage is that the feedback lecture requires extensive planning and preparation (Osterman, Christensen, and Coffey 1985).

A second alternative, the "guided lecture" (Kelly and Holmes 1979), was devised to help students develop the capability to successfully synthesize lecture material while taking notes. After students are given the objectives of the lecture, they are asked to put their pencils down and to *listen* carefully to a lecture approximately one-half of the class period in length (25 to 30 minutes), attempting to determine the major concepts presented and to remember as much supporting data as possible. At the end of the lecture, students are instructed to spend five minutes recording in their notes all that they can recall. The next step involves students in small discussion groups reconstructing the lecture conceptually with supporting data. At this juncture, students prepare their complete lecture notes, using the instructor to resolve questions as they arise. Students are encouraged to reflect on the lecture later that same day and to write in narrative form, without reference to the lecture notes, the major concepts and most pertinent information presented. Although no evaluative data were presented, the authors believe that the guided lecture improves students' skills in listening and synthesizing information. Others' experience using the guided lecture in the classroom and in faculty development workshops suggests that the method is indeed successful. Individuals enjoy the cooperative interaction, and the collective experience provides them with notes that are superior to those produced individually.

Student-Generated Questions

To supplement resource-based learning modules, the "responsive lecture" was developed to meet the needs of individual learners by providing feedback over material covered in the course (Cowan 1984). One class period per week was devoted to answering open-ended, student-generated questions on any aspect of the course. A few rules applied. All topics had to be couched as questions. Although everyone could submit questions, they had to explain briefly why they considered the question important. The class then ordered the questions in terms of general interest, and the instructor lectured on as many topics as time allowed. Students' response to the technique was overwhelmingly positive, although the approach is not for the faint-hearted, as the instructor has no control over, and therefore may lack expertise in, the topics students want discussed. To counteract this drawback, faculty might try other, more structured approaches. For instance, students could submit written questions before the next class period, a technique suitable for reviewing lecture material and outside readings (Gleason 1986).

Are Large Classes a Special Case?

Anyone who has taught a large class is aware of the physical and emotional constraints upon both instructor and students. The situation is impersonal—perhaps even overpowering—when students fill hundreds of seats rising tier after tier in a large amphitheater that seemingly dwarfs the instructor. It is not surprising that, in these circumstances, professors who might otherwise use methods encouraging active learning revert to presenting formal 50-minute lectures without significant discussion.

A study of the interactions in large classrooms of 19 faculty in the colleges of business, natural sciences, engineering, and liberal arts at the University of Texas–Austin noted 14 categories of classroom interaction every three seconds (Lewis and Woodward 1984). The authors found that, across all disciplines, "teacher talk" categories filled 88 percent of the class time and "student talk" categories only 5 percent of class time. Silence accounted for approximately 6 percent of the remaining time. Slight variations occurred: Instructors in liberal arts involved their students more than other instructors, approximately 7 percent of the time, but hardly an overwhelming amount of participation. Instructors in the natural sciences had the highest "teacher talk" figure, 92 percent. These data empirically support the notion that instructors in large classes overwhelmingly lecture. Further, the small amount of interaction that does occur in large classes might be of little substantive value. One analysis using large medical education classes found that significantly less interaction occurred at the levels of analysis, synthesis, and evaluation in classes with more than 16 students. Seventy-one percent of interactions were at the lowest level: memorization of knowledge (Mahler, Neumann, and Tamir 1986).

In the past, these circumstances were usually mitigated by the belief that students would typically have the opportunity to ask questions and seek clarification of course material in an accompanying discussion led by a teaching assistant. This case apparently is not necessarily true. One extensive survey of introductory economics courses in 518 institutions in the United States found that in very large classes (more than 125 students) 48 percent of the schools surveyed had *no* discussion classes to supplement their large lectures. In schools with classes of 35 to 125, 95 percent of those surveyed did not provide discussion classes (Sweeney et al. 1983). Many economists, therefore, cannot expect that alternative methods of teaching will supplement what they do in the large lecture hall. Indeed, such figures could represent a much wider phenomenon in many disciplines.

Research indicates that the large classroom can still provide a fertile ground for instruction if traditional lecturing techniques are modified. Students' negative attitudes toward large classes can be changed if an instructor clearly outlines the objectives of the course and uses a variety of instructional strategies with an emphasis upon the use of visual media

(Moore 1977). Similarly, an earlier meta-analysis of 500 experimental studies on the teaching of writing found that structured classes with clear objectives and interaction that focused on specific problems students encountered in writing were more effective than classes dominated by the instructor in which students were passive recipients (Lewis, Woodward, and Bell 1988). The validity of these results was tested by comparing four small lecture classes with one large class characterized by active learning (Lewis and Woodward 1984). The amount of interaction between instructors and students was analyzed by the expanded Cognitive Interaction Analysis System (CIAS), and students' learning was evaluated by a pre- and posttest that had been checked for validity of contents and reliability in grading. The analysis showed that the one large communication class did indeed involve less lecturing and more participation by students than the smaller classes. Results of the final examination showed that students in small classes scored better on the objective test but that students in the large, active-learning class scored higher in the categories of small-group presentations, writing reports, writing letters, individual oral presentations, and average final scores. The study also produced another interesting result that supports the necessity for teaching higher-order thinking. Averages on tests in the smaller classes correlated with the average percentage of "analysis-level" questions asked by the instructors. The greater the number of higher-level thought questions, the higher the students' scores on the posttest, leading to the conclusion that active learning is effective and that the method of instruction used, *not size of the class,* seems to be the major ingredient of learning.

The problem is how to deal effectively with large classrooms and vast numbers of students. Several possible solutions have been derived from the literature on communication (Gleason 1986). First, because large space hampers communication between teacher and student and among students, the instructor can create the perception of a smaller space by arriving before class and talking to students, moving around during class sessions, and personally returning exams and distributing handouts to students. Such actions send the message that the large lecture hall need not be a deterrent to frequent personal interaction. Further, a large room filled with strangers creates an impersonal atmosphere that diminishes the sense of personal responsibility students feel toward their instructor or fellow students (Gleason 1986). Instructors must make an effort to create a supportive climate, perhaps by learning as many students' names as possible, by adding personal comments to selected tests or quizzes, and by recognizing students in class whenever an opportunity arises.

Because large classes decrease the possibility of individual participation, some instructors ask for written questions, while others successfully use various options for holding discussions with a small portion of the students in the class. For example, an area can be set aside for those who want to volunteer as discussants on a given day, or students can be notified in advance that they will sit in a given area and discuss specified material. Further, because large rooms make the instructor appear distant and unapproachable, an instructor must "get personal" and establish a climate of humanness by openly admitting when material becomes confusing or interjecting humor where appropriate (Gleason 1986). Indeed, one of the most powerful tools for establishing rapport between student and instructor is the ability to laugh at oneself.

Last, the spatial configuration of large classrooms (particularly amphitheaters) emphasizes the role of students as spectators. The obvious and effective solution is also quite simple: Get students involved in active learning both in and out of the classroom. For instance, one professor at Pennsylvania State University has adopted the concept of a "quality circle," meeting with students to evaluate past classes and to review possible options for future classes. A resourceful instructor can use each of these techniques to break down the natural barriers in communication large classrooms impose.

In a similar fashion, a provocative and compelling overview of how one instructor has successfully implemented strategies promoting active learning in large classes for a number of years starts with three basic assumptions: (1) a teacher should use a variety of instructional strategies on different days and within any given class period; (2) visual reinforcements are necessary to focus students' attention and to reinforce material that is presented; and (3) students learn best when they are asked to provide personal insights and interpretations (Frederick 1987). Several strategies can be used to achieve these goals:

1. An interactive lecture can begin with students brainstorming what "they know or think they know" about a given topic while the teacher (or a fellow student) writes all contributions on the board. The instructor then uses these contributions from students to build a conceptual framework for the topic under discussion and to correct any apparent misconceptions. A variation on this approach is to develop a problem-solving lecture, setting the stage with a minilecture and then engaging the students in possible solutions to the issue or problem raised.

2. Questioning can take many forms, ranging from standard open-ended questions to having groups of two or three students work together first to contemplate a judgment question and then to build a response from the group based on specific information or evidence presented in the course. The length of the exercise depends upon the complexity of the question.

3. Small groups can provide energy and interaction, but the size of the group is best determined by the size of the class, its physical arrangement, and the task. Three points help to improve the quality of small-group work: The instructions given to students must be explicit; an appropriate time frame must be chosen and communicated; and a group recorder should be assigned the responsibility for providing feedback during debriefing.

4. A large class also offers a good opportunity to "practice an old-fashioned but woefully ignored technique: explication de texte" (p. 53). By reading and analyzing passages from the text out loud, students can learn higher-order thinking skills, that "criticism" is a legitimate intellectual exercise without the excessive emotionalism commonly associated with the term. The technique also is applicable to alternative sources of information, such as analytical curves or works of art.

5. It is even possible to use large lecture settings for debate among students based on simulations and role playing. After providing a minilecture to establish a proper setting, the instructor divides the class into two or more large groups, each with a well-defined role to play in the problem. The groups are then given a concrete task and asked to develop a position or to describe a course of action. If the problem is developed correctly, the groups' positions should provide alternative or opposing viewpoints

that lend themselves to debate. People representing a group's position are then asked to participate in whatever format the instructor deems most appropriate: role playing, panel discussion, formal debate, and so on. These approaches demand careful planning and an instructor's willingness to relinquish control. Although the results are sometimes not as erudite as might be desired, with practice and feedback these alternative strategies can energize even a large classroom (Frederick 1987).

Strategies involving active learning can be used to modify the traditional lecture in a classroom of any size. The instructional method chosen should be based upon the faculty member's personal preference and the strategy's suitability for meeting the specific objectives for that class period. The remainder of this monograph explores many of these alternative strategies in greater depth.

*For an observer, staying out of a discussion is almost as
hard as sitting through a lecture* (Eble 1976, p. 55).

Although the most common way for professors to engage students in active learning is by stimulating a discussion, the
technique is not universally admired.

*One should always be aware that when one invites discus-
sion, very likely one is covering for one's own inadequacy.
There should never be any doubt that discussion in a university is the vacuum that fills the vacuum. When one runs
out of material, one can always fill the gap by inviting questions and having an interchange* (Galbraith 1987, p. 3).

When the objectives of a course are for students to retain
information after the end of the course, to be able to apply
knowledge to new situations, to change students' attitudes,
to motivate students toward further learning in the subject
area, or to develop students' problem-solving or thinking
skills, however, then discussion is preferable to lecture
(McKeachie et al. 1986). Further, a thoughtful analysis suggests that group inquiry is based upon recognized principles
of learning, including the necessity for students to develop
their own answers, the fact that students are most likely to
think when they are asked to write and speak, and the fact
that students learn best when they work in concert with other
students (Kraft 1985). To achieve these goals, a good discussion takes careful planning, thoughtful implementation, and
a supportive classroom environment, and requires an instructor's knowledge of techniques of questioning and strategies
and styles for involving discussion.

A Supportive Classroom Environment
Although little research has been done on discussions in
actual college or university classrooms, one way to ascertain
the elements that constitute a supportive environment is to
look at the specific behaviors that students rate most highly
on their evaluations of instructors. A number of studies show
a fairly consistent pattern. For example, classroom behaviors
falling into two general categories are highly correlated with
students' ratings of teachers' effectiveness (Erdle, Murray, and
Rushton 1985). First are those behaviors or characteristics that
convey enthusiasm and/or rapport and thereby result in stu-

dents' interest and participation. Grouped under the label "charismatic" are such things as speaking clearly, relating material to students' interests, and moving and gesturing. The second category, "organizational" skills, includes "giving a preliminary overview, stating objectives, and using headings" (p. 395). Instructors who want to improve their classroom teaching can readily learn and adopt these behaviors.

Creating a supportive classroom environment involves more than merely having the skills that encourage students to participate and learn in the classroom. More important, instructors must create an intellectual and emotional climate that encourages students' taking risks. A list of behaviors that promote interpersonal rapport by projecting warmth, openness, predictability, and a focus on student-centered teaching, based on observations of 25 "superb" professors in the classroom, includes:

- Being strongly interested in students as individuals and highly sensitive to "subtle messages from them about the way they feel about the material or its presentation";
- Acknowledging "students' feelings about . . . class assignments or policy and encouraging them to express [those] feelings";
- Encouraging students to ask questions and being "eager for them to express personal viewpoints";
- Communicating "both openly and subtly that each student's understanding of the material is important to him or her";
- Encouraging "students to be creative and independent in dealing with the material [and] to formulate their own views" (Lowman 1984, p. 17).

At the other end of the spectrum are behaviors all but guaranteed to stifle discussion in the classroom: The instructor fails to recognize students as individuals, uses sarcasm, is upset or preoccupied when students ask questions, is defensive about policies or procedures, and is inconsistent or unpredictable. All instructors interested in skillfully using the discussion method should create their own list of behaviors they can use to develop a nurturing classroom environment.

Perhaps the single most important act that faculty can do to improve the climate in the classroom is to learn students' names. Among many other benefits, doing so acknowledges the decentralization of authority in the classroom and rec-ognizes the increased responsibility of students for their learn-ing and the learning of others. In addition, to involve a greater number of nonparticipants in class discussion requires a means of recognizing all students—and pointing at someone is awkward at best. While the authors know of no empirical research on the impact of learning names on students' behav-ior in the classroom and learning material, anecdotal evidence strongly supports this practice. Simple yet effective ways to do so include:

1. Learn students' names from class rosters and then try to match names with faces.
2. Ask students to provide biographical information on index cards to help personalize the memorization of names and faces.
3. Distribute papers (quizzes, tests, and assignments) directly to each student.
4. Require students to visit in the office early in the semester.

Students will appreciate the effort, even if the instructor is unable to learn all the names.

Discussion Material

Even a cursory glance at general works on leading classroom discussion reveals that one key element is frequently glossed over as authors move on to introducing specific strategies and skills for leading discussions. Very little attention has been paid to the requirements of *what is going to be discussed,* even though the selection of subject material is of paramount importance to developing a successful discussion. The mate-rial must, for example, first be of interest to both the instructor and the students. Although some have denigrated the Socratic method as being too directive, one element of Socrates's teaching is worth noting: His lessons concerned topics that interested his students (Hoover 1980). Good discussion lead-ers constantly search for appropriate materials to spark responses from students and carefully hoard materials that have worked successfully in the past. Second, good reading selections must be complex enough to engender different points of view regarding the issues or problems presented. If they contain a little controversy, so much the better. Last, the materials should be self-contained and relatively brief so

If they contain a little controversy, so much the better.

that they can be presented to students during class time. Although assigning outside reading for future discussion might work in an upper-division or graduate class, what instructor has not failed in the effort to create a vibrant discussion over "the reading"? Taking time in class to develop a common base of experience is one way to reduce greatly the risks associated with discussion; it is well worth the time invested.

A variety of materials and techniques can be used to trigger discussion. Traditionally, literature has focused on the use of materials in many shapes and forms: essays, speeches, poems, specific data, tables, figures, and so on. Other useful stimuli to promote lively discussions include surveys of students or self-assessment questionnaires that serve as a basis for determining differences among students' attitudes or values. Many of the interactive techniques discussed in the next section are especially suitable as triggers: audiovisual materials, writing activities, case studies, problems, debates, drama, role playing, and simulations. Each can provide varied experiences that will stimulate discussion among students.

Types of Questions

Although many instructors state that a combination of lecture and discussion characterizes their classrooms, a study of questioning in colleges and universities indicates that the true use of discussions is probably not very extensive (Ellner and Barnes 1983). The results of videotaping and coding interactions in the classrooms of 40 full-time undergraduate faculty at both large and small institutions provide some fascinating insights into the dynamics of college classrooms. The mean percentage of total class time spent with students answering questions from the professor was less than 4 percent. Of those questions, using the Aschner-Gallagher system of coding, 63 percent were memory questions (recalling specific data) and 19 percent were routine administrative questions. Thus, only 18 percent of the questions required higher-order thinking. Moreover, when the sequence of questioning was analyzed, nearly one-third of the questions asked did not receive a response from students. These findings held true regardless of the school's size, the discipline, or the course level.

Effective questioners know the different types of questions that can be asked and when it is most appropriate to ask them. Although a variety of classification systems can be used, perhaps the most commonly used divides questions into four categories: (1) cognitive memory questions (Who was president of Iraq in 1990?); (2) questions that call for convergent thinking (If war broke out in the Middle East, what would happen to the price of oil?); (3) questions that call for divergent thinking (Under those circumstances, what political and military options would be open to the United States?); and (4) evaluative questions (What would be the best response to an Iraqi invasion of Kuwait?). Unfortunately, most teachers operate only at the first level as they conduct a recitation (drill, review, quiz) to determine the extent of students' knowledge about assigned content. In fact, a review of the literature found no essential difference in the types of questions that teachers had asked over a 50-year period (Gall 1970). "About 60 percent of teachers' questions require students to recall facts; about 20 percent require students to think; and the remaining 20 percent are procedural" (p. 713). Later research simply validated this statement (Ellner and Barnes 1983).

In an effort to break out of these circumstances, the Maryland State Department of Education (McTighe 1985) issued the following useful guide of question types based on cognitive levels (Bloom et al. 1956):

Knowledge: Identification and recall of information
    Who, what, when, where, how..................?
    Describe......................................
Comprehension: Organization and selection of facts and ideas
    Retell......................................
Application: Use of facts, rules, and principles
    How is.....an example of....................?
    How is.......related to......................?
    Why is............................significant?
Analysis: Separation of a whole into component parts
    What are the parts or features of..............?
    Classify..........according to...................
    Outline/diagram................................
    How does........compare/contrast with.......?
    What evidence can you list for................?
Synthesis: Combination of ideas to form a new whole
    What would you predict/infer from.............?
    What ideas can you add to....................?

How would you create/design a new............?
What might happen if you combined............?
What solutions would you suggest for.........?
Evaluation: Development of opinions, judgments, or
decisions
Do you agree...............................?
What do you think about.....................?
What is the most important...................?
Place the following in order of priority............
How would you decide about...................?
What criteria would you use to assess.........?

A caveat about questioning is necessary. Students are not
guaranteed to respond at the same cognitive level as that of
the question posed. For instance, when asked to compare and
contrast the strengths and weaknesses of the North and the
South before the Civil War, students could conceivably
(indeed likely) respond with material memorized from a similar discussion presented in the assigned reading. Thus, they
would be responding at the knowledge level to a question
designed to stimulate analytic reasoning.

An exploration of the verbal structure of questions to see
which question forms are most effective used videotapes of
classroom interaction to evaluate the number of statements
students make, the number of participating students, the number of student-follows-student sequences, and the total time
students talked (Andrews 1980). Based on these variables,
the researcher concluded that the three most productive types
of questions were structured variations of a divergent question. In terms of effectiveness, with the most effective first,
they are the playground question, the brainstorm question,
and the focal question.

1. *The playground question.* Such a question is structured
   by the instructor's designating a carefully chosen aspect
   of the material (the "playground") for intensive study.
   ("Let's see whether we can make any generalizations
   about the play as a whole from the nature of the open-
   ing lines.")
2. *The brainstorm question.* The structure of this type of
   question is thematic. Participants are encouraged to generate as many ideas on a single topic as possible within
   a short space of time, but the theme defines the range

of what is appropriate. ("What kinds of things is Hamlet questioning—not just in his soliloquy but throughout the whole play?")

3. *The focal question.* This type of question focuses on a well-articulated issue. Students are asked to choose among a limited number of positions or viewpoints and to support their views in discussion. ("Is Ivan Illych a victim of his society, or did he create his problems by his own choices?")

Questions that were less successful, according to the data, were those that were too broad or vague and therefore confused students, those that asked several subquestions at once, those that were so convergent that students perceived only one answer was "right" and therefore hesitated to respond, and those that were factually oriented with one answer.

Effective Techniques of Questioning

Several recommendations, all based on research, have been proposed for asking questions in the classroom (Wilen 1986, p. 10):

- *Plan key questions to provide structure and direction to the lesson.* Good discussion questions must be carefully focused on the objectives for the class period. Useful questioning strategies for five different types of discussion could include a sequence of questions for what is called "a predicting discussion" (Hyman 1980, pp. 45–46):

  1. *What are the essential features and conditions of this situation?*
  2. *Given this situation . . . , what do you think will happen as a result of it?*
  3. *What facts and generalizations support your prediction?*
  4. *What other things might happen as a result of this situation?*
  5. *If the predicted situation occurs, what will happen next?*
  6. *Based on the information and predictions before us, what are the probable consequences you now see?*
  7. *What will lead us from the current situation to the one you've predicted?*

  In using this approach, some spontaneous questions will evolve based on students' responses, but the overall direction of the discussion has largely been planned.

- *Phrase questions clearly and specifically.* Avoid vague or ambiguous questions, such as "What did you learn from the reading?" or "What about the main character of the story?" Clarity increases the probability that students will respond effectively.
- *Adapt questions to the level of students' abilities.* Questions should be framed simply, using a vocabulary that is appropriate for the students in the class. When students cannot understand a question, they do not answer it.
- *Ask questions logically and sequentially.* Random questions confuse students and reflect a lack of planning, while a sequential set of questions provides coherence and more effectively promotes students' understanding.
- *Ask questions at various levels.* One approach suggests asking questions requiring cognitive memory to establish an initial base for further discussion. Higher-level questions can then be posed to illustrate the lesson's objectives.
- *Follow up on students' responses.* Teachers can elicit longer and more meaningful statements from students if they simply maintain a "deliberative silence" after an initial response (Dillon 1984). Too often, teachers ask rapid-fire questions, one after another, a circumstance more like an interrogation than a discussion. Other appropriate actions can draw out students after an initial response: make a declarative statement, make a reflective statement giving a sense of what the student has said, declare perplexity over the response, invite the student to elaborate, encourage other students to raise questions about the issue at hand, or encourage students to ask questions if they are having trouble.
- *Give students time to think when responding.* The single most important action a teacher can take after asking a question is simply to keep quiet. An analysis of the patterns of interaction between teachers and students in hundreds of classrooms found that teachers averaged *less than one second of silence* before repeating or reemphasizing material, or asking a second question (Rowe 1974). Under such circumstances, it is no wonder that students remain silent. Training teachers to wait silently for three to five seconds after asking a question achieved significant benefits: The length of students' responses, the number of appropriate but unsolicited responses, exchanges

between students, questions from students, and higher-level responses all increased, and the number of students' failures to respond decreased. Waiting three to five seconds, however, can seem like an eternity.

That is the time it takes . . . to chant "Baa baa black sheep, have you any wool?" while seeing [whether] the student has any more to offer. If you hold out for the full three seconds, the student will hand over "three bags full" (Dillon 1987, p. 63).

- *Use questions (and techniques) that encourage wide participation from students.* Try to involve everyone in the class by asking questions, even of nonvolunteers. Pay attention to the level of difficulty of the questions asked, however, to elicit the best possible response. The goal is to provide opportunities for everyone to participate; frequent individual successes will ultimately empower even the most hesitant students to jump in.
- *Encourage questions from students.* Create a supportive environment that allows risk taking and then encourage students to ask questions. They will respond.

Discussion Strategies and Style

Students need to be eased into the discussion process in stages because most have not had significant prior experiences with successful discussions (Bligh 1986). Instructors can constructively set the tone for the semester by having students work on a relevant discussion task the very first day of class. The instructor should clearly state expectations for students' involvement, and the task must be simple enough that students can both understand the problem and solve it successfully. In these early stages, it is preferable to ask students to work individually on an answer for two minutes and then to have them share their responses with a small group. After an appropriate interval of time, depending on the difficulty of the question (three to five minutes), the small groups report to the class as a whole. In later sessions, after students have become comfortable with each other and the process of discussion, they can successfully work in larger groups with a minimum of supervision. As an evolutionary process, this approach minimizes risk for both the students and the instructor. "The basic rule in teaching by discussion methods is 'Start

It is difficult for most instructors to release control.

with small groups, for short periods with simple tasks. Then gradually increase the size, length, and difficulty'" (Bligh 1986, p. 19).

Successful discussions, however, depend on far more than mere technique. "What is essential is the teacher's attitudes, dispositions, and commitments to classroom discussion . . ." (Dillon 1984, p. 54). These attitudes and dispositions are particularly relevant to the difficult challenge of developing a personal style for leading discussions. An extensive in-service training program conducted in Great Britain found that teachers who enrolled in a seminar to learn techniques for leading discussions expected the seminar leaders to use a directive, didactic style. They were disconcerted when they found they had to participate in meetings with shared responsibilities; when they returned to their classrooms, many reported a tendency to "slip back into a didactic teaching style" (p. 54). This account suggests the difficulty that faces all instructors—and students—who have experienced only teacher-centered classrooms. It is difficult for most instructors to release control. Every instructor, even those committed to and experienced with active learning, must continually ask, "Did I dominate the discussion today?" Otherwise, students might write of experiences similar to this one:

He asks us questions and then answers them himself. At the beginning of the course we all waved our hands in the air like fools. No more. We get in there, put on our pleasant masks, and go to sleep (Tiberius 1990 p. 99).

For a successful discussion to take place, therefore, instructors must determine their objectives for the class period, structure questions that are appropriate for the material under consideration, and then demonstrate techniques designed to extend students while maintaining a supportive environment. The catalog of St. John's College restates these principles more eloquently. Professors (referred to as "tutors") are expected to:

. . . be good questioners, able to raise important issues that will engage the intellectual and imaginative powers of their students. Next, they must be good listeners, able to determine the difficulties of their students and to help them to reformulate their observations and examine their opinions. The

*tutors should be ready to supply helpful examples and to
encourage students to examine the implications of their first
attempts at understanding. In summary, the role of the
tutors is to question, to listen, and to help . . . [,] but first
of all the tutors will call on the students to try to help themselves* (Myers 1988, p. 44).[1]

---

1. Those who have problems living up to this ideal are well advised to consult
Small Group Teaching: A Trouble-Shooting Guide (Tiberius 1990).

ADDITIONAL STRATEGIES PROMOTING ACTIVE LEARNING

Creativity has sometimes been called the combining of seem-ingly disparate parts into a functioning and useful whole (Adams 1974, p. 25).

Thus far, the active learning strategies discussed are variations of conventional classroom methods. These traditional approaches are those that college and university faculty find most familiar and use most often. A wide variety of additional techniques promoting active learning are available, however, that have proven to be effective in promoting students' achievement, in enhancing students' motivation, and in changing students' attitudes. Creative instructors will become familiar with the strengths and weaknesses of the strategies discussed in the following paragraphs so that they can be blended into a "useful whole."

Visual-Based Instruction

In the past, many have claimed that no teaching method has held out more promise for revolutionizing the classroom than visual-based instruction. As each new technology—still projection (slides, filmstrips, or overhead transparencies), film, multimedia presentations, television, and video—has been introduced into the classroom, proponents announced that the millennium was here (Siegfried and Fels 1979). Unfortunately, evidence from research to demonstrate the effectiveness of visual-based instruction upon learning outcomes has proven to be very elusive. For instance, an extensive review of the literature synthesizing results of 74 separate studies of visual-based instruction in the college classroom found that, in comparison to conventional teaching (presumably lecturing), students' achievement increased only slightly when visual-based techniques were used and that even this advantage was less pronounced when the same instructor taught both classes (Cohen, Ebeling, and Kulik 1981). When used as a platform for delivering content, therefore, visual-based instruction has not yet been shown to be significantly better than lecturing—perhaps because simply viewing a 50-minute film or videotape does not actively involve students any more than listening to a 50-minute lecture.

Visual-based instruction did appear to have a significant impact, however, when used as a source of feedback for training teachers or the acquisition of skills such as typing, sewing, or athletics (Cohen, Ebeling, and Kulik 1981). More recent studies suggest that this same effect may apply to laboratory classes. For instance, in a biology class at Drake University, students viewed videotapes of dissections that they were to perform later in a comparative anatomy laboratory. Although test scores were not significantly different from classes taught by conventional means, students' performance in the laboratory gained perceptibly. The frustration of working with unfamiliar specimens diminished, and the quality of dissections greatly improved (Rogers 1987). Similarly, the use of interactive videodiscs to simulate chemistry laboratory experiments has proven successful. Students' achievement using the interactive videodiscs was significantly higher than students' achievement who performed traditional laboratory experiments on the same material (Smith, Jones, and Waugh 1986).

Another meta-analysis of the literature on research found that the use of motion pictures, television, videotaped recordings, and still media in nursing education, coupled with opportunities for responses from students (active learning), produced a significant positive change in students' attitudes and retention (Schermer 1988). The study suggests the importance of using media as the focal point for interactive techniques. Rather than simply serving as a substitute for a content lecture, however, media are best used as triggers for such activities as class discussion about the special significance of the content or as the basis of a short analytical essay about the implications of the events shown. For instance, the Dutch State School of Translation and Interpreting uses an English-language video on the greenhouse effect as the focal point for analytical discussions on both the scientific concepts presented and the speech patterns of academicians and reporters (Kleerx 1990). This simple exercise is a classic example of the instructional power inherent in the media. In one classroom in The Netherlands, Dutch students had the opportunity to watch global events and to listen as several British scientists discussed one of the 20th century's most pressing environmental issues. Similarly, in the United States, students' awareness of social issues can be powerfully heightened by a simple slide show depicting conditions in the urban ghetto or showing the plight of Native Americans at the end of the 19th century. Few faculty who remember the televised news broadcasts from Southeast Asia in the 1960s and 1970s can deny the dramatic power visual images had upon college students' thoughts, discussions, and political actions.

Although the media can be a valuable tool for developing strategies promoting active learning, many faculty resist the use of this technology in their classrooms. Indeed, one colleague steadfastly argues that his 1,000 words are better than any picture, suggesting that a study in the 1960s on resistance to instructional television in higher education seems apropos even today.

> *[The professor who is vehemently against the innovation] perceives himself as being highly competent in his chosen profession, and thus spends more time doing what he thinks he does best—teaching by traditional methods. He sees as the greatest threat those forces within his environment [that] might "dilute" the academic aspects of the university or alter his role within it* (Evans and Leppmann 1967, p. 90).

Students might also resist learning from media because of their views toward its efficacy. While students typically attribute great difficulty to learning from computers, many perceive that television is "shallow" and "easy" (Clark 1983, p. 455). Although the media have high potential, their actual acceptance and use in the classroom have been significantly less than its proponents have envisioned.

Writing in Class

Having students write in class as an adjunct to other teaching strategies is a relatively new phenomenon that has been promoted by a national movement, Writing across the Curriculum. By academic year 1987–88, proponents of students' writing had been successful in creating writing programs at 38 percent of institutions of higher education in the United States (Watkins 1990b). Typically, such programs encourage instructors in all disciplines to incorporate a wide variety of writing tasks into their classroom presentations. Such tasks might include keeping journals, focusing thoughts on a particular topic, summarizing a lecture or assigned reading, or composing an essay describing the solution to a problem presented in class.

A considerable body of literature documents that writing in class has several positive benefits for students and instructors. Keeping a journal, for instance, allows students to explore their values and to express their feelings. The method can also provide instructors of all disciplines with insight into the level of students' comprehension of conceptual material. According to one student:

Today I just received my test grade and I felt really good because I got an 82 and I thought it paid off for all my studying. I think this creative writing helps you for the test. It also improves your writing (Ambron 1987, p. 264).

This excerpt reflects a common theme found in the literature. Many have stated that writing assignments, regardless of type and whether or not the instructor evaluates them, improve students' writing skills and learning subject matter. In one study at Montana State University, 88 percent of the students surveyed thought that writing essays had improved their understanding of physics (Kirkpatrick and Pittendrigh 1984). Indeed, the concept that "writing is a way of learning more about every subject" is one of the fundamental assumptions about the Writing across the Curriculum movement (Young and Fulwiler 1986, p. 29).

Current research suggests that those who have extolled the value of all kinds of writing to promote learning in the classroom may have been overenthusiastic—or at least premature. For instance, some evidence has questioned the assertion that simply assigning more writing to students automatically leads to improved writing skills. A study of the hypothesis that the more writing students were asked to do the more their skills would improve found that, while the scores of the control group remained essentially constant during the semester, posttest scores *declined* in eight out of 11 classes that emphasized writing, reflecting a decrease in either skills or motivation during the period studied (Day 1989). A significant positive correlation was found between students' achievement scores and how thoroughly an instructor marked papers for spelling, grammar, content, and logic. Conversely, students showed a significant decline in writing scores when instructors graded only the first page of their work.

In a study of the effect that systematic assignments would have on writing skills, students were given weekly essay tests from a larger set of questions previously made available to them so that they could organize, write, and revise practice answers (Madigan and Brosamer 1990). Essay tests were then graded for content and skill in writing. The final examination in the course consisted of the same question that had been used in the second weekly quiz. Much to the researchers' surprise, the students did *not* show statistically significant improvement when answering the question a second time. The results of a later, revised experiment were similarly interesting. When students were provided with specific rhetorical patterns as models (exemplification, definition, comparison and contrast, and process analysis), given repeated opportunities for practice, and provided feedback, their writing skills did improve significantly. In short, considerable explicit instruction was needed before students provided documented evidence of improvement.

The results of research on whether writing improves students' learning course content also is mixed. Students in a foreign policy class that focused on writing did not show significantly improved achievement compared to a control group on either the objective or essay components of a major examination (Michalak 1989). Other studies have shown that writing essays does not increase immediate recall of content in comparison to taking notes, writing short answers, focused thought, or outlining (Hinkle and Hinkle 1990; Newell 1984). A different study, however, was able to differentiate the effects of different writing tasks on the immediate and delayed recall of content (Langer and Applebee 1987). When students were asked to read and study (but not write), respond in writing to 20 short-answer questions, write a summary, or write an analytic essay, the researchers found that those who wrote did better on recalling overall information than those who just read and studied and that those who wrote analytical essays grasped the gist of the passages more readily than those using the other approaches. Recall of specific information was mixed, depending upon the difficulty of the passages being read. The authors concluded that instructors should assign note taking, comprehension questions, and summarizing tasks if the goal is to review a general body of specific information, and analytical essays if the goal is to focus students' attention on concepts and relationships.

These studies indicate that writing in class is a valuable strategy promoting active learning when it has been tied to explicit goals of the course and other appropriate instructional methods. It also appears that no quick fixes are available; to improve students' skill in writing still requires instructors' significant effort as they carefully plan objectives, provide repeated opportunities for practice, and provide time-consuming feedback and coaching.

Problem Solving

A variety of techniques for solving problems have been based on a decision-making model espoused by John Dewey (1924). The process has four steps: (1) defining a problem; (2) diagnosing possible reasons for the problem; (3) searching for alternative solutions; and (4) evaluating the alternatives and choosing the most appropriate solution. This schema has served as the basis for two popular instructional approaches to solving problems—case studies and Guided Design.

Case studies

Since their introduction at Harvard Law School in the 19th century, case studies have been used in a number of disciplines across the academic spectrum. A case study, which can be defined as "the factual account of human experience centered in a problem or issue faced by a person, a group of persons, or an organization" (Fisher 1978, p. 262), can range from a highly structured exercise to a very unstructured problem that could raise a variety of complex issues and alternative solutions. Typically, case studies are written objectively and include a brief overview of the situation along with descriptive information that both establishes a context for the problem and identifies the major decisions that must be made.

The following example of a case study describes a short incident that could serve as the basis for analysis and discussion in class.

> *As the new academic vice president of a large community college, you have decided to implement a merit salary program to reward equitably those faculty members who are doing the best job. Your deans, although sympathetic to your cause, cannot agree on how most fairly to assess faculty performance . . . , not to mention whether merit increases should be the only reward for outstanding service. At their request, you are meeting with them tomorrow to clarify your new policy and give them guidelines. How do you prepare?* (Fisher 1978, p. 270).

Although this method has traditionally been used in graduate-level instruction, it can also be effective at the under-graduate level if cases are presented carefully within students' experiential framework. The approaches the instructor takes can vary, depending on the number of participants (individual or group), the type of analysis used (analytical processing, role playing, dramatization, or discussion), the order of analysis required of the class (chronological or simultaneous), and the degree of structure imposed (Romm and Mahler 1986).

Empirically, case studies have proven to have several advantages as a strategy promoting active learning. Because they are based on real-life incidents, case studies that incorporate role playing allow students to vicariously experience situations in the classroom that they might face in the future and thus help bridge the gap between theory and practice. Moreover, the decision-making model for case studies both fosters higher-order thinking and sends a clear message to students that real problems have no "right" or "wrong" answers (Romm and Mahler 1986). Case studies also have other advantages. By dealing with the human emotions inherent in the situations described, the cases usually capture students' interest and are highly motivational (Hoover 1980). This affective involvement leads to one of the most important advantages of case studies: changes in attitudes. Although little evaluative data exist on the case study method, one study involving academic deans and vice presidents compared, under controlled conditions, the case study method with an approach involving position papers and seminars. The results show that the use of case studies was significantly more effective in bringing about a change in attitudes on the part of participants (Fisher 1978). Finally, if the physical facilities available are appropriate for discussion, using case studies is cost effective: At Harvard it has been used in groups containing 80 students (Christensen and Hansen 1987).

Certain disadvantages are associated with case studies, not the least of which is the perceived role of the instructor in this—or any other—process involving active learning. The teacher using case studies must be willing to relinquish some control in the classroom, as increased emphasis is placed on promoting students' *learning*. Old habits are hard to break, however.

By dealing with the human emotions inherent in the situations described, the cases usually capture students' interest and are highly motivational.

*It's intellectual chaos and so darned inefficient! Why let
a class "muck around" for an hour trying to work through
a point when I can explain it in a few minutes. They call
that teaching?* (Christensen and Hansen 1987, p. 30).

Students also could have problems with the approach. Not
only must they possess or cultivate the ability to present their
point of view in an articulate fashion and to listen to others—
skills that many find intimidating—they are often uncomfortable with the inherent ambiguity and the lack of rigid structure in the classroom (Paget 1988; Romney 1984; Watkins
1990a). If instructors can accept the role of facilitator and are
willing to invest sufficient time to allow students to develop
the necessary skills, however, the case study method can be
very rewarding.

Guided Design
Guided Design, developed at West Virginia University in the
late 1970s, is based on a modified decision-making model
that explores solutions to open-ended problems. The process
has several essential steps:

1. Stating the problem and establishing a goal;
2. Gathering relevant information;
3. Generating possible solutions to the problem;
4. Listing constraints on what can be accomplished;
5. Choosing a possible solution;
6. Analyzing the important factors that must be considered
   in the development of a detailed solution;
7. Creating (synthesizing) a detailed solution;
8. Evaluating the final solution; and
9. Recommending an appropriate course of action (Wales
   and Nardi 1982).

Guided Design formalizes the steps that one often takes
unconsciously in making everyday decisions. An illustrative
example of this approach considers the question, "Where shall
we eat tonight?" (Wales and Nardi 1982). Using the steps of
Guided Design, the response would include stating the goal
(to acquire food), generating possible solutions (what kinds
of restaurants are available?), and considering the constraints
(how many people are going? what are the costs involved?
how much time is available? what transportation will be

required?). Once a choice is reached, steps 6 through 8 would be applied where appropriate and a recommendation made. The formalization of this kind of process helps students become more intentional and skillful when solving problems.

Although Guided Design has numerous advocates and has been implemented in most undergraduate disciplines, relatively little research has studied its effect on students' learning. One study compared test results of Guided Design sections with control groups that had received the same content in lectures. The classes using Guided Design scored substantially higher on the test items, but the results included no description of the instrument used or statistical data (Coscarelli and White 1982). A two-semester sequence of Guided Design courses introduced in the freshman engineering program at West Virginia University appeared to be particularly effective in terms of retention rates and grade point averages at graduation (Wales 1979). Like case studies, Guided Design therefore appears to be a useful approach for teaching problem solving.

Computer-Based Instruction

One of the fastest-growing areas in instructional innovation and technology involves the use of computers, either in the classroom or in associated laboratory settings. Although most institutions seem overwhelmed by increasing demands for the latest computer hardware and software, schools are only beginning to assess whether the high costs of educational computing are justified by students' increased achievement (Johnston and Gardner 1989). The answer seems to be a qualified "yes."

Researchers at the University of Michigan have constructed meta-analyses of the effectiveness of computer education in schools from the elementary to collegiate levels. Typically, computers are used for routine drill and practice, for managing data, for word processing, or for programming information. Their studies found that computer-based instruction (CBI) had several positive features. First, students in CBI classes generally learned more: Based on 199 studies, students' average achievement rose from the 50th to the 61st percentile. Second, compared to those taught traditionally, students learned their lessons in two-thirds of the time. Third, students liked their classes more when they received help on the computer. And last, students in CBI developed more positive attitudes toward computers, an attribute that will become increasingly important as society incorporates more technology into all aspects of work and home life. Computer-based instruction might have fared so well in evaluative studies, however, because instruction was well designed and was presented in an "attractive and engaging way" (Kulik and Kulik 1986; Kulik and Kulik 1987, p. 7). The inference, of course, is that traditional instruction might fare better if it also were well designed and attractively presented.

Apparently, CBI can affect students with different learning styles. One study in mathematics found that, although the achievement scores of all students in the experimental sections and all students who received traditional instruction did not differ significantly, those students who were field-dependent (they are less analytical than field-independent students) performed significantly better in the math sections that were supplemented by computer instruction. Thus, "students with dissimilar cognitive styles achieve differently as a result of learning environments" (MacGregor, Shapiro, and Niemiec 1988, p. 462).

Anecdotal evidence suggests other positive attributes of CBI. Biology classes at the University of Michigan incorporate tutorial programs into the course of study. As a result, students' achievement has increased, particularly among those who have deficient backgrounds in science. At Eastern Michigan State University, students in an astronomy class are able to see a visual simulation of the motion of the planets on monitors as their professor lectures. In the botany department, other students are able to analyze field data and work numbers so efficiently that they can investigate more variables in less time. In addition, employers pay more for computer skills that are adjunct to another degree. Interior design majors with a minor in computer-assisted design, for example, are able to command a starting salary that is $10,000 higher than other graduates from their department (Johnston and Gardner 1989).

Computer-based instruction does have its limitations, however. For instance, the costs of computing can be very high for those schools that establish institutionwide computer systems. The start-up cost for a public computing cluster at the University of Michigan containing 189 computers was $768,000, with an additional $189,000 annually (including maintenance, utilities, replacement, supplies, and personnel).

Average figures per computer across five dissimilar institutions ranged from $2,000 to $4,000 for initial start-up and $900 to $1,300 for annual operating costs. Much of this expense entailed replacement costs for obsolescent computers, because technology in the field is moving so rapidly that what appears to be adequate at the time of purchase can be thoroughly outdated within three to four years. An additional hidden expense for computer operations is faculty time. One biologist reported that he took four years to finish computer programs for the departmental introductory course, a project that he had estimated could be completed in a six-month sabbatical (Johnston and Gardner 1989).

Computerizing a campus will also run into resistance from administrators and faculty. One dean left a new computer designated for his office sitting in its packing carton for months "because he had no need for it." Moreover, the recurring issue of course content versus instructional process will keep some faculty from introducing computers in the classroom. A recent survey of finance departments in the California State University system found that 33 percent of the professors stated they did not use computers because "the subject coverage of the course does not allow time . . ." (Ma 1989, p. 71). Whatever the stated reason, many will resist computerization because they are uncomfortable with new technology.

Cooperative Learning
The goals of cooperative learning are twofold: to enhance students' learning and to develop students' social skills like decision making, conflict management, and communication. To achieve these goals, proponents have over the past two decades developed classroom strategies that emphasize small groups of students working together in a structured process to solve an academic task. The duration of the project can be anywhere from one class period to a whole semester. Although cooperative learning has been employed primarily in kindergarten through grade 12 in the past, it recently has gained favor in colleges and universities (Cooper 1990).

The sociology classes of two instructors at Illinois State University exemplify a cooperative learning situation. Cooperative learning is regularly incorporated into 70-minute classes of 15 to 50 students. At the beginning of the semester, groups of four to six students are created by random assignment. To ensure that students are prepared for the day's discussion, a worksheet containing three to five questions is distributed before the scheduled group session. These questions can be designed to prepare students for examinations, written assignments, or research projects, or simply to structure the discussion. To deal with the vexing problem of "freeloaders," each student must submit written answers to the worksheet as a requirement for participating in the group's discussion. (Instructors examine individual worksheets later to ensure compliance.) To handle procedural questions, the group elects a new leader and a new recorder for every discussion session; their responsibilities are carefully laid out in an instruction sheet. During the discussion, each group produces a written report containing such features as major ideas expressed, points of disagreement within the group, and a brief summary of those points about which the group reached consensus. Groups are given 45 to 50 minutes to complete their reports; the reassembled class then compares and contrasts their findings. Finally, grades are assigned to the report developed in class, and all members of the group share that grade (Rau and Heyl 1990).

Grading is the most vexing issue associated with cooperative work in any active learning situation (Cohen 1986). One meta-analysis of students' achievement in cooperative classrooms from kindergarten through grade 12 differentiated between incentives given to individuals based on their performance, incentives given to the group based on individual performances, or incentives given to the group as a whole based on a single product. The author concluded that a group award for individual achievements led to the most statistically significant learning among students. Operationally, it is determined by averaging the average scores of members of the group on an assessment of individual learning, such as a quiz. Thus, the concept of individual accountability within the group—"two or more individuals are interdependent for a reward they will share if they are successful as a group"—is at the heart of cooperative learning (Slavin 1983, p. 431).

Such an approach flies in the face of decades of individualized, highly competitive educational practices. One proponent of cooperative learning suggests that grading the group should constitute only "a very small amount of the total grade . . ." (Cooper 1990, p. 1). To support this position, one study at a university showed that students working cooperatively in a structured process significantly increased the accuracy of their short-term recall answers over students working individually using their own study methods. The use of structured study also had a small but significant transfer effect on subsequent individual performance (Lambiotte et al. 1987).

Even if there were no significant difference in achievement between cooperative learning techniques and traditional methods, many would argue persuasively that the other benefits of cooperative learning justify its use. For instance, when one professor switched from lecturing to a cooperative classroom, an absentee rate that had been nearly 50 percent fell to only 1 percent. Similarly, studies have shown that cooperative learning has strong positive effects on race relations, self-esteem, and a willingness to cooperate in other settings (Slavin 1983). Given these characteristics, it would appear that cooperative learning is a strategy that might appeal to many professors; it certainly warrants further research in a university setting.

Debates

The format for a debate can range from the formal presentation of opposing sides with a chance for rebuttal to less formal situations where the presentation of arguments for both sides serves as the basis for discussion in class. Regardless of the format, debates have several benefits for students, including possibly reducing the bias an instructor might bring to the course, forcing students to deal with their own biases, enhancing students' skill in research, promoting logical thinking, increasing skill in oral communication, and motivating students (Schroeder and Ebert 1983). Some evidence even suggests that debates prove as valuable to those students who listen as to those who actually participate (Moeller 1985).

A survey of 175 business managers reported in 1983 that strong communication skills were considered the most important skill that business majors could acquire in college. To meet this need, the use of debates has proven successful in upper-division business courses (Combs and Bourne 1989). Students' confidence in their speaking ability increased significantly after participating in a series of debates, and over 70 percent of the students in those courses wished that other business courses would use the same format. Nearly 80 percent believed that the use of debates provided them with a better understanding of both sides of the issues presented. Finally, 66 percent of the students believed they had learned more from the course than if the material had been presented in a lecture.

Although debate often works best with controversial issues, it has been used successfully in a large math class involving 100 first-year students. The instructor organized scientific statements generated by students and then placed them on the board without evaluation. After the class discussed the validity of the statements (by proof, refutation, counterexample, and so on), students individually committed themselves to a position by casting a vote for or against each proposition. When the discussion was brought to a close, validated statements became theorems; those found incorrect were preserved as "false statements," and appropriate counterexamples were presented. A questionnaire at the end of the course found that 75 percent of the students preferred the incorporation of debates into the class, as long as the instructor provided appropriate minilectures to introduce and summarize the discussions (Alibert 1988).

Drama

Evidence indicates that the use of plays in the classroom promotes students' enthusiasm toward the content and increases their learning. (For purposes of clarification, plays and drama are defined as those performances that use written scripts, as opposed to activities like role playing, which typically are more spontaneous.) An experiment to evaluate drama as a method for teaching research principles to graduate students in social work focused on a play entitled *The Experiment*. The script was designed to allay students' fears about research methods by providing role models who explored difficult concepts in conversational language. The play, presented by student volunteers, then served as a vehicle for discussion in class based on study questions that explored specific content and attitudes. When the study compared the play's presentation with a lecture that covered the same material, students liked the drama significantly more than the lecture. And students exposed to the play retained more information as measured by an immediate posttest, although no difference was apparent in material remembered one week later. Thus, drama enhanced the experience in the classroom (Whiteman and Nielsen 1986).

Drama can also become a vehicle for students' interaction with conceptual material and content as a play unfolds. In one business and technical writing class, a series of skits were designed to be interrupted so that students in the class could supply appropriate dialogue for the situation presented or could evaluate and discuss specific comments made by members of the cast. Although the skits greatly enlivened the classes, they served a much more useful purpose. Because the plays were focused on specific problems inherent in the material and were an integral part of the course, the students' interaction provided an opportunity for the instructors to evaluate the students' grasp of the conceptual material. Further, like other interactive techniques of this type, drama gave students "a better sense of what it means to write for real readers for real business reasons" (McCoy and Roedel 1985, p. 11).

Role Playing, Simulations, and Games

Role plays, simulations, and games can be used to help students experience "stressful, unfamiliar, complex, or controversial situations" by creating circumstances that are momentarily real, thereby letting students develop and practice those skills necessary for coping (Davison 1984, p. 91). They also promote working in groups, usually generate high levels of motivation and enthusiasm, provide credit for personal initiative, and can run parallel to lectures that explicate the material and issues under consideration (Cloke 1987). Role playing and simulations/games, which often overlap, have not been clearly defined in the associated literature, but in this monograph, role playing is defined as sessions that last less than an hour, while simulations and games can last several hours or even days. Further, simulations and games (which can include role playing) are defined more precisely than are role plays (which often are spontaneous) and include guiding principles, specific rules, and structured relationships. Role plays in particular can be effective in forcing students to examine their attitudes toward other people and circumstances. They also have an advantage in that no special equipment or materials are needed.

Role playing has been used in a variety of settings, from elementary schools to graduate, professional training. Role plays are usually short, spontaneous presentations, although they can be longer, more elaborate productions where participants have diligently researched their role's background before the presentation. Usually the teacher's function is to structure the situation by providing background details and a general sketch of the roles to be played, to share with the audience the specific goals of the role play so that they can observe and then participate in the ensuing discussion, to serve as a facilitator as the role play develops, and to guide the evaluation of the role play and to restate or summarize pertinent developments (Lachs 1984).

At Harvard Law School, role playing forms the basis for a semester-long course in business law in which students have the opportunity to develop skills in interviewing, counseling, and negotiating. Weekly activities in the course are carefully structured so that all students are actively involved in the developing scenario, which highlights the conflicting interests of a small manufacturer and his partner, a wealthy grocer who has invested in the business. Students in the role play prepare a memorandum in advance of class, detailing their plans for each meeting, which includes an analysis of all relevant legal doctrines and the pertinent facts. Members of the class not involved in the role play that week are motivated—and involved—because they must hand in brief commentaries analyzing the memoranda provided by the players. As a final project at the end of the course, pairs of students are asked to negotiate a written agreement resolving the dispute between the partners. Grades are based on the quality of class participation and the written materials submitted (Herwitz 1987).

One of the more innovative—and personally risky—methods of role playing involves a lecturer debating himself. A professor of political science has found that arguing two or more sides of an issue can pique students' interest. During his first venture into role playing, he wore a red, white, and blue straw hat to extol the virtues of the U.S. political system, covering all the points he would normally have included in a lecture. Then he donned a beret and vigorously presented the case for the French party system. Vehement rebuttals followed until the conclusion of the debate, whereupon students burst into applause. Somewhat chagrined at his own enthusiasm, the professor remained skeptical about how much learning had taken place, but two events occurred: Students asked for a return of the hats, stating that he had given his best lecture of the year, and students' responses on the next test on the U.S. two-party system were far more insightful than their efforts on any other questions. The method has been refined over the years to include greater participation by students. They are encouraged to challenge the position represented by "the hat," and the instructor replies in character. This approach exemplifies one of the strengths of role playing: Students can criticize the role being portrayed without feeling threatened. Similarly, the instructor's responses challenging their statements are not perceived as disparaging students' comments. In follow-up questionnaires, a high percentage of the students found the debates about the role plays more interesting than traditional lectures and believed that they had learned more, both in content and in an understanding of different points of view (Duncombe and Heikkinen 1989).

Although simulations and games have become increasingly popular in universities, research provides mixed results as to their relative effectiveness. A review of studies of business simulations and games between 1973 and 1983 found that many of the projects were flawed because they did not report sufficient information to allow replication or were limited in their generalizability because they failed to consider the many variables inherent in simulations and games (practices in the classroom, size of the teams, complexity of the game, and so on). Nonetheless, students usually expressed positive feelings about the experiences, and several studies found an increase in students' achievement (Wolfe 1985).

One of the more innovative— and personally risky— methods of role playing involves a lecturer debating himself.

One interesting study in economics has demonstrated the usefulness of simulations and games for reaching students with alternative learning styles. Under controlled conditions, 120 students were randomly assigned to four class sections: Two sections were taught by lecture/discussion, and two sections included lecture, discussion, simulations, and games. The researcher hypothesized that subscores from a questionnaire about learning styles could be used to classify students into two groups: (1) students thought more likely to profit from simulations and games because they obtained meaning from *spoken* information, could place themselves in another person's position, and could be influenced by peers, in contrast to (2) students more likely to learn best from the lecture/discussion method because they obtained meaning from *written* information, were self-directed, and made their own decisions (Fraas 1982). Students' performance at the end of the semester was correlated on the basis of these characteristics and the sections assigned. With a student's final grade as a measure of performance, the results indicated that, although neither method was superior to the other as an approach for teaching the economics survey course, the characteristics of learning style chosen did produce a statistically significant difference in performance, depending upon which class the student was enrolled in.

Students responsive to simulation techniques (as determined by the questionnaire on learning style) in the experimental classes received higher grades than their counterparts in the control classes; conversely, students responsive to lecture/discussion methods recorded higher grades in the control classes than their counterparts in the experimental classes (Fraas 1982, p. 1).

This study provides empirical support for the common assertion that instructors should use a variety of teaching methods to successfully reach students with different learning styles. One can also infer that reliance upon a single method of teaching within the classroom will penalize students with an alternative learning style!

Peer Teaching

Although peer teaching, often called peer tutoring, has existed in some form since the latter part of the 18th century, its appearance in higher education has been a relatively new phenomenon. Peer teachers have been classified into five groups: (1) teaching assistants, both graduate and undergraduate; (2) peer tutors, who work with students one on one in an academic area; (3) peer counselors, who advise students over a broad range of academic concerns; (4) partnerships, that is, one-to-one relationships where each partner alternates in the role of teacher and student; and (5) working groups, which work collectively to enhance individual performance (Whitman 1988). Of these types, partnerships and working groups promote the use of active learning in the classroom.

One of the earliest uses of partnerships occurred at McGill University, where pairs of students were organized into "learning cells." In a structured format, students would individually prepare for class by reading an assignment and generating questions focused on the major points or issues raised, be assigned randomly to pairs at each class meeting, alternately ask questions of each other and provide corrective feedback on a response where necessary, and receive coaching from an instructor who moved from pair to pair. A variation of the procedure consisted of having each student read different selections and then teach the essence of the material to his or her partner (Goldschmid and Goldschmid 1976).

The effectiveness of learning cells was evaluated against three other options (seminars, discussion, and independent study) in a large psychology course. Students working in pairs scored significantly higher on achievement tests and preferred the approach over other methods. These results were replicated in various classes across other disciplines at McGill University; they showed that learning cells were significantly effective, regardless of class size, class level, or the nature of the subject matter (Goldschmid and Goldschmid 1976).

Partnerships and groups have also been used effectively in writing courses. At Westfield State College in Massachusetts, for example, freshmen students taking a critical thinking course were required to edit other students' papers, making comments and approving each section. The process of peer editing acted to have students become involved in the reality of an academic environment (Whitman 1988, p. 26).

Similarly, in English classes at Sweden's University of Linköping, groups of students brainstormed ideas about a given topic and, after they created first drafts individually, critiqued other students' work. Whether students work in pairs or in groups, such activities have several advantages: (1) Teachers spend less time editing; (2) students are apt to pay more attention to comments from peers; (3) in group work, students gain a sense of a wider audience; (4) students' attitudes toward writing can be enhanced by socially supportive peers; and (5) students learn more about writing and revising by having to critically read others' successive drafts. It should be noted, however, that although students seem to strongly support the involvement of peers in writing, they do have some reservations about the process. Students were hesitant about their own capabilities to edit papers, fearing they lacked the expertise necessary and might provide incorrect suggestions. Some students were afraid they might hurt others' feelings (Davies and Omberg 1986).

Although most of the research on peer teaching has focused on peer tutoring in elementary and secondary schools, the findings from those studies presumably can be generalized to college settings. One meta-analysis found that students' achievement was significant in a typical peer tutoring class: "The average child in the tutored group scored at the 66th percentile of the students in the untutored or control group" (Cohen, Kulik, and Kulik 1982, p. 241). The findings also indicate that achievement was higher in more structured programs and that students developed more positive attitudes toward the subjects in which they were tutored. Not surprisingly, the tutor also accrued significant benefits from the process of teaching others. Explaining conceptual relationships to others forced tutors to refine their own understanding. These findings would be particularly appropriate for college and university peer tutoring programs in which upperclass students are used as teaching assistants in courses that they themselves have recently taken.

For the instructor who would like to go beyond the traditional methods of lecturing and discussion, a number of effective strategies promoting active learning are available to choose from. If a faculty member is hesitant about selecting one of these techniques because some question exists about its comparative effectiveness with the lecture, he or she should consider the following. When delivering course content, as the research indicates, many of these approaches have little or no demonstrated advantage over the lecture. It is equally true, however, that most of these strategies have been shown to deliver content *as well as lectures* while providing diverse presentations that enhance students' motivation and achievement.

BARRIERS TO CHANGE IN THE CLASSROOM

The spirit of America is innovation. In almost every area of life we crave the new and better. . . . Yet college teaching stands out as one of the few fields in which innovation and improvement are neglected (Eurich 1964, p. 49).

In light of the recent calls for significant educational reform in higher education and the consistent recommendations urging the use of active learning in the classroom, a vital issue that demands examination is "Why do faculty resist change?" Scholarly writing and research into this important question can be subdivided into two categories: (1) faculty resistance to change in general and (2) faculty resistance to the use of strategies promoting active learning in particular. Before examining each one, however, it is important to remember that this monograph has been designed to provide a descriptive, analytic account of why faculty have not eagerly embraced recommendations to employ active learning, not as an exercise in faculty bashing. An analysis of common obstacles and barriers to academic change, it is hoped, will better enable readers to understand and act upon the suggestions and strategies for change proposed in the next section.

Global Barriers to Change

Six common barriers to professors' changing have been identified:

1. The professional setting in which faculty work tends to be stable.
2. A professor's sense of professional definition tends to resist change.
3. The feedback circle in the classroom tends to be stable (that is, students and faculty share consistent expectations about each other's role in the classroom).
4. Trying something new arouses inevitable feelings of discomfort or anxiety.
5. Faculty can become self-enchanted as they think aloud and lecture.
6. Faculty see few incentives to change (that is, deviation from established methods invites risk but offers relatively few rewards) (Ekroth 1990).

The stability of the situation

A fundamental paradox exists about research in teaching and learning in higher education:

> *On the one hand, we are vitally concerned with exploring
> the unknown, with challenging every old principle, and with
> finding new knowledge in our fields of specialization. On
> the other hand, we accept wholly the traditional methods
> or old wives' tales about teaching without any thought of
> improving our procedures* (Eurich 1964, p. 51).

Similarly:

> *Teaching-learning arrangements have been taken for
> granted, for the most part, throughout the history of higher
> education; the instructional procedures and approaches
> of today are much the same as those of yesteryear* (Milton
> 1968, p. 1).

For many faculty, then, things are the way they are today because that is the way they have always been; further, most faculty find the majority of traditional teaching practices more
comfortable than not.

The editor of the widely read *Teaching Professor* newsletter
tells of sitting in on the first class session of a one-credit
course required for all teaching assistants in the college of
engineering at a large research university and overhearing
a student say, "Geez, why do I have to be here? I've already
taught for three semesters" (Weimer 1989, p. 1). (Her response to this statement was, "This begins my 18th year in
the college teaching profession, and I seriously wonder if I
know enough about teaching to do even a half-way respect-
able job this year.") This anecdote illustrates the powerful
and enduring belief—passed on from generation to generation—that there is little to learn about college teaching.

The self-definition of professors
Expectations about faculty members' roles and responsibilities
often are categorized into three areas: teaching, research, and
service. Though institutional contexts and climates naturally
vary, currently on many campuses considerable tension exists
regarding the relative importance that should be placed on
each (Boyer 1987). "The language of the academy is reveal-
ing: Professors speak of teaching *loads* and research *opportunities,* never the reverse (Association of American Colleges
1985, p. 10). Further:

*The greatest paradox of academic work in America is that
most professors teach most of the time, and large proportions
of them teach all of the time, but teaching is not the activity
most rewarded by the academic profession nor most valued
by the system at large. Trustees and administrators in one
sector after another praise teaching and reward research.
Professors themselves do the one and acclaim the other*
(Clark 1987, pp. 98–99).

Regardless of the relative value campuses place on each, these
three categories provide faculty members with the universally
recognized cornerstones for personal self-definition—and
the same three categories create inherently conflicting pressures for faculty members' attention, time, and energy. To the
extent that campuses provide greater recognition and rewards
for research over teaching, the likelihood of faculty members'
seriously and significantly making efforts to improve instruction is reduced.

With respect to one's responsibilities for teaching in the
classroom, faculty universally "know" that their institution
expects excellence in teaching, but relatively few campuses
have critically examined and discussed explicitly how "excellence" is best achieved and assessed. Research has shown that
faculty perceptions about the elements most closely associated with "superior teaching" clearly place "knowledge of
the subject matter" well above all other considerations. For
example, faculty view the professor's task as transmitting
knowledge and skills (Blackburn et al. 1980). A provocative
analysis of metaphors about teaching and learning in higher
education describes the "Container-Dispenser model" (Pollio
1987). Knowledge is a substance, material, or source of power,
instructors are containers (filled with content, material, and
facts), and students are vessels (wanting to be filled up).

Knowledge (the substance) is often rendered as a food *the
instructor* spoon feeds *or just* feeds *to students, who so* cram
for exams that they are no longer hungry *for knowledge.
Students may be requested to* regurgitate *facts on an examination. If the professor* dispenses *knowledge, he or she
becomes a* fountain *of information who asks you to* spout
*facts on a test. . . . The teacher (as dispenser) gives infor-
mation, puts it into your head, throws out ideas, or may
even hand it to you on a* silver platter. *The student, as con-*

tainer, may soak up *or* absorb *facts,* store *information; if the student does none of the [m], he or she is likely to be* empty-headed, *or just plain* vacuous" (Pollio 1987, p. 13).

It seems apparent that faculty whose view of teaching and learning can be represented by the Container-Dispenser model would be especially concerned about covering content. If it is the only goal, then skillful lecturing can readily be understood as an important means to this end.

The feedback circle in the classroom

Faculty and students share many expectations regarding the proper role that each plays in teaching and learning, those perceptions having been formed in traditional classroom settings. For instance, many professors are very specific about how they learned to teach, "model[ing] themselves after powerful presences from their own student days" (Eble 1983, p. 1). Yet, of thousands of faculty members, few can point to a powerful role model in their past who consistently and skillfully used active learning in the classroom. For this reason, if no other, it is not surprising that professors rarely use strategies promoting active learning.

Students' resistance is another element of the feedback circle. Some students will always resist the use of active learning because it provides a strange and dramatic contrast to the more familiar passive listening role to which they have become accustomed. Listening to faculty talk is not only a more familiar role for students; it is also a considerably easier one! Research using the Grasha-Riechmann Student Learning Styles Scales has revealed that students whose preferred learning styles are "avoidant" and/or "dependent" typically favor lectures over active involvement (Fuhrmann and Grasha 1983). Through both verbal and nonverbal means, such students often communicate their displeasure with nontraditional instructional approaches; professors' selective perception of students' unpleasant reaction then encourages the use of more traditional teaching methods.

Other research on the differences in students' learning styles (Claxton and Murrell 1987) and on stages of students' intellectual development (Belenky et al. 1986; Perry 1968) is worthy of mention. Kolb's Experiential Learning Model, for example, can be used to provide a conceptual framework for understanding students' positive or negative reactions to strategies promoting active learning (Svinicki and Dixon 1987). Faculty can expect that, in any classroom, some students will prefer to be receivers (observers or listeners), while others will prefer to be active participants.

A classic work on students' intellectual and ethical development suggests that "dualist learners" want structured lectures in which faculty describe clearly and precisely what they need to know (Perry 1968). Such students expect instructors to maintain control over the class and to simply present the facts; they believe that a student's job is to pay attention, to take notes, and to memorize the facts. Dualists typically find class discussions confusing and a "waste of time." It is only in a later stage of intellectual development—the relativism period—that students take greater responsibility for their own learning, view class participation as an exciting opportunity to exchange differing perspectives, and become willing to teach and critique each other. Similarly, parallel studies of women identify the contrasting positions of students seeking "received knowledge" (who sit with pencils poised, waiting to write down an instructor's every word) from those interested in "connected learning" or trying to view the world from the perspective of another in a nonjudgmental fashion (Belenky et al. 1986). Together, these studies point to one unmistakable conclusion: Faculty who employ active learning in their classrooms are unlikely to please all of their students all of the time. But neither do faculty who rely regularly on traditional lectures.

Feelings of discomfort and anxiety
Experiencing some degree of discomfort and anxiety in response to one's initial attempts to try something new is probably a universal trait—not unlike the feeling when one first tries to roller skate or to ride a two-wheel bicycle. So it is when faculty consider trying new and different ways of acting in the classroom. For example, an important study of faculty resistance to instructional television reports that university professors "tend to be conservative, favoring old, tried-and-true methods and viewing innovations of any kind with considerable apprehension" (Evans and Leppmann 1967, p. 55). Though the empirical data are now 25 years old, little evidence exists in the literature on innovation in higher education to suggest that this portrait of university professors has changed greatly in recent years.

The self-enchantment of faculty

Classroom sessions have been observed in which, class after class, the teacher repeatedly does all the work (Weimer 1989). Indeed, any faculty member who has ever attempted to lead a true 50-minute class discussion where students primarily talk and respond to one another knows how difficult it is to keep from interrupting students.

Unfortunately, while faculty may become enchanted listeners to their own lectures, students do not always share this same passion.

At a freshman psychology lecture we attended, 300 students were still finding seats when the professor started talking. "Today," he said into the microphone, "we will continue our discussion of learning." He might as well have been addressing a crowd in a Greyhound bus terminal. Like commuters marking time until their next departure, students in this class alternately read the newspaper, flipped through a paperback novel, or propped their feet on the chairs ahead of them, staring into space. Only when the professor defined a term [that], he said, "might appear on an exam" did they look up and start taking notes (Boyer 1987, p. 140).

The lack of incentives to change

Faculty see few incentives to change for several common reasons. First and foremost is the pervasive belief that "we are all good teachers." In a survey of 24 campuses, for example, between 20 and 30 percent of the faculty rated their own teaching as "superior," between 58 and 72 percent rated their own teaching as "above average," between 7 and 14 percent rated their own teaching as "average," between 0 and 3 percent rated their own teaching as "acceptable," and between 0 and less than 1 percent rated their own teaching as "poor" (Blackburn et al. 1980). A colleague has astutely interpreted these data to mean that 90 percent of the faculty who describe their teaching as "above average" illustrate clearly higher education's version of the "Lake Wobegon Effect" (referring to Garrison Keillor's fictional town in Minnesota in which "*all* the women are strong, and *all* the men are good looking, and *all* the children are above average"). When one's self-perception includes the image of being an above-average teacher, little reason exists to try new approaches.

And despite the large number of reports that have been critical of higher education, it appears that campus reward systems have changed little over the years. Faculty perceptions about college/university reward structures indicate that they have remained stable over time (Blackburn et al. 1980). By not providing clear and visible rewards for innovative teaching, institutions have implicitly endorsed the status quo of classroom instruction.

"People are often shocked that teachers should require tangible incentives to try a new innovation" (House 1974, p. 73). Further, the "personal costs of trying new innovations are often high," and "innovations are acts of faith," requiring "that one believe that they will ultimately bear fruit and be worth the personal investment, often without the hope of an immediate return" (p. 73). Given that most faculty view themselves as above average, that there are few financial incentives to change, and that change can involve high personal costs, faculty who attempt alternatives to traditional approaches are relatively few.

Barriers to the Use of Active Learning
While many faculty agree that true learning requires active participation, in workshop settings these same faculty describe why they do not make greater use of strategies promoting active learning in their classrooms. Several obstacles are commonly mentioned:

1. One cannot cover as much content in the time available;
2. Devising strategies promoting active learning takes too much preparation before class;
3. Large classes prevent implementation of such strategies; and
4. Materials or equipment needed to support active learning are lacking.

Covering the content
A short yet telling conversation between one student and his math lecturer illustrates the pressure instructors feel to cover the content required for a course. The student asked, "Sir, could you explain that last step?" to which the instructor replied, "If you're going to interrupt me with questions, we'll never be able to cover the material" (Janes and Hauer 1987,

". . . and all the children are above average."

p. 36). Though this sad dialogue admittedly illustrates a rather extreme case, all faculty feel some pressure to cover the content of their course or discipline. Because the use of active learning reduces the amount of time available, faculty conclude that lecturing is an easier and more efficient means of transmitting information. One implicit assumption that should be challenged, however, is the unstated conviction that the way to best facilitate students' learning is through the oral presentation of course material. "As has been pointed out countless times, the lecture was outmoded by the invention of printing and by cheap and easy access to printed works" (Eble 1976, p. 43). Further:

> *In terms of content, there is little a lecturer can say [that] she or he cannot write more concisely. What makes a course more than the sum of the readings on which it is based is the social experience: the sets of relationships between teacher and students and students with one another* (Eisenberg 1987, p. 18).

Moreover, faculty who regularly use strategies promoting active learning typically find other ways to ensure that students learn the assigned content (for example, using reading and writing assignments or classroom examinations). One way to help promote students' success in such efforts is to provide explicit, discipline-specific training in study skills in the context of ongoing activities (Davies 1983; Eison 1988). Another helpful strategy involves the preparation of self-instructional materials for students' use (Bedient, Garoian, and Englert 1984). When students are able to master successfully course material through their own efforts, a large number report that they do not want their instructors to cover the same material in class. Research exploring students' orientations toward learning and grades conducted with over 5,000 students on seven campuses found that between 28 and 57 percent of those surveyed reported becoming "annoyed when lectures or class presentations are only rehashes of easy reading assignments" (Eison and Pollio 1989, p. 13). Between 87 and 92 percent of these students reported, however, that they "enjoy classes in which the instructor attempts to relate material to concerns beyond the classroom" (p. 13). These findings suggest that to serve best the expressed preferences of a sizable number of students, faculty need not feel compelled to spend all or most of the time in class covering information that was previously covered in assigned readings.[2]

Preparation for class

An examination of faculty resistance to innovation notes that, in general, the level of resistance experienced is related to the amount of time and energy required to learn new skills or roles (House 1974). Further, new skills can make old skills obsolete, and both concerns are powerful influences on faculty attitudes and behaviors. Most faculty the authors have met in workshops, for example, believe that the amount of preparation time needed before class to implement strategies promoting active learning is greater than that needed to update or revise existing lectures. And many instructors fear that the use of active learning requires the immediate and total revision of all class notes for every class they teach.

As countless faculty advise students on the first day of class, learning any new body of knowledge or mastering any set of new skills requires an investment of time and energy. The validity of this educational truism is equally appropriate for faculty contemplating any significant change in instructional approaches. Once the decision to employ active learning has been made, however, the actual amount of preparation time and energy needed for implementing the strategies is neither excessive nor unreasonable. Further, the use of strategies promoting active learning can be gradually introduced into an instructional repertoire. One helpful suggestion is to select a single course to work with, perhaps beginning with the course one teaches most often and is most familiar with, rather than attempting to change several courses simultaneously.

Large classes

While students, parents, or faculty generally do not take kindly to the use of large classes, the temptation to allow class sizes to increase has mounted with budgetary pressures (Weimer 1987). While large classes might preclude the use of some strategies promoting active learning (for example, students'

---

2. Perhaps "uncovering the material" by actively involving students in the process of learning information might be a more appealing metaphor for many educators than the picture of "covering the material" through traditional lectures.

---

presentations or frequent papers), they certainly do not prevent the use of *all* possibilities. Moreover, students' reactions to large classes depend more upon the quality of instruction than the actual class size; survey findings from over 800 University of Washington undergraduates reveal that 41 percent of the students actually preferred classes with enrollments of 100 students or more (Wulff, Nyquist, and Abbott 1987).

The lack of materials, equipment, or funds
The lack of materials or equipment needed to support active learning can be a barrier to the use of some strategies promoting active learning (for example, demonstration and laboratory exercises or computer- and visual-based instructional activities) but certainly not all. The majority of the strategies discussed earlier require little expense. For example, asking students to summarize in writing the material they have read or forming pairs to evaluate statements or assertions requires no equipment.

Risk: The Greatest Barrier of All

"To understand the adoption and transformation of innovative ideas in the classroom, one must also understand the phenomenology of the teacher's world . . ." (House 1974, p. 79). A crucial concern in the phenomenology of the professor's universe is one's willingness to face two types of risks: those involving how students will react to the use of active learning and those involving how faculty members feel about their own teaching.

With regard to the first, the risk is that students will not participate actively, learn sufficient content, or use higher-order thinking skills. For instance, along with an instructor's decision to use active learning in the classroom often comes the nagging fear, "What if my students don't want to participate actively?" Indeed, many faculty have reported that students' passivity has become an increasing problem in their classrooms. A somewhat more puzzling issue is the common fear among faculty that students will not learn as much content when they use strategies promoting active learning. Based on the literature on active learning summarized previously, however, students learn as much or more when alternatives to traditional lectures are used.

Developing instructional strategies to help students learn to think creatively and critically has become recognized as one of the most pressing educational challenges facing faculty today. On this subject, the advice of the experts is clear: Students will not learn how to successfully perform these skills by listening to lectures that attempt to "model" these difficult intellectual tasks.

> *If instead of focusing all our interest on the teacher—What shall I teach? How can I prove that I have taught it? How can I "cover" all that I should teach?—we focused our interest on the student, the questions and the issues would all be different. Suppose we asked, what are his purposes in this course, what does he wish to learn, how can we facilitate his learning and growth? A very different type of education would ensue* (Carl Rogers 1951, cited in Bligh 1986, pp. 170–71).

Faculty members also risk not feeling in control of the class, not possessing the needed skills, or being viewed by others as not teaching in an established fashion. For example, little doubt remains about who is in control of the traditional classroom when a faculty member lectures. Before class the skillful lecturer selects specific objectives for the class session, carefully organizes the presentation's content, identifies illustrations, and possibly shares some jokes or humorous anecdotes. During class the instructor typically does most of the talking, decides when to ask specific questions of students, determines when to pause for students' questions, and selects the material noted on the blackboard. In short, the instructor is in charge of it all. When active learning is used, the instructor shares control with the students. For some, this risk is significant; for others, it might be the most difficult task of all. Students might challenge the instructor's authority (the class might get out of hand) or competency (asking a question for which no ready answer is available). A faculty member's ability to relinquish control and share power in the classroom can enable students to become actors playing major roles in their own education rather than being an audience listening and learning from a great performer on center stage.

As noted earlier, active learning requires faculty to learn new skills, in turn entailing further risk. The amount of time and energy required to learn new skills or roles can be dramatically reduced, however, by referring to references cited throughout this text. Moreover, most fields of study in higher education have one or more journals devoted to the sharing of disciplined-based pedagogical techniques. Many helpful suggestions for the successful use of strategies promoting active learning can be found in current issues of such journals. In addition, those teaching introductory courses should consult journals in secondary education as well.

Like most professionals, faculty members typically seek the favorable regard of colleagues and peers, especially in the academy because it is one's colleagues and peers who serve on promotion and tenure committees. Because the use of strategies promoting active learning deviates from well-established norms, one always runs the risk that such behavior will not be viewed as "good" teaching. Research on innovation, for example, has shown that:

> *the most innovative member of a system is often perceived as a deviant from the social system, and he or she is accorded a somewhat dubious status of low credibility by the average members of the system* (Rogers 1983, p. 27).

"The myth that they won't let me" (Combs 1979) is a common response from faculty to calls for reform in education. While readers may know of instances to the contrary:

> *All of us . . . have far more freedom to innovate than we like to believe. The myth that they won't let me is really a handy excuse for inaction. It even has advantages. Instead of having to blame ourselves for inaction, we can see ourselves as really splendid persons who would do great things if only we were allowed to do so. . . . Teachers have far more freedom to innovate than they ever use. When the classroom door is closed, nobody, but nobody, knows what is going on in there except the teacher and the students. . . . Teachers may not be able to change the educational system, or their administrator, but the variations possible within an ordinary classroom are almost limitless* (Combs 1979, pp. 209, 212).

The final section describes how this change might be achieved.

CONCLUSIONS AND RECOMMENDATIONS

One must learn by doing the thing,
for though you think you know it—
you have no certainty, until you try
(Sophocles, cited in Rogers 1983, p. 163).

How can the barriers and obstacles to the incorporation of strategies promoting active learning in the classroom be overcome? Exploring answers to this all-important question is the focus of this final section. As is often the case when attempting to analyze complex issues or to resolve difficult problems, a multidimensional approach is proposed. In particular, the section considers steps that can, and should, be taken by college and university faculty, faculty developers, campus administrators, and educational researchers.

The Role of College and University Faculty

The biggest and longest-lasting reform of undergraduate education will come when individual faculty or small groups of instructors adopt the view of themselves as reformers within their immediate sphere of influence, the classes they teach every day (Cross 1989, p. 1). One way faculty members can begin to reform undergraduate education is through the use of strategies promoting active learning in the classroom. To do so successfully, each must personally confront the issue of taking risks discussed in the previous section. Though active learning will always involve some level of risk for faculty, by carefully selecting strategies that are at a personally comfortable level of risk, an instructor can maximize his or her likelihood of success.

The different types of strategies promoting active learning described earlier vary in the level and type of risk each involves. One conceptualization, contrasting characteristics associated with low- and high-risk strategies, can be seen in table 1 (Eison and Bonwell 1988). In terms of class time, relatively short strategies involve considerably less risk than those activities involving greater class time. For example, when students meet in small discussion groups to analyze an issue or to solve a problem for 10 to 15 minutes, less risk is involved that valuable class time will be nonproductive than when they meet in discussion groups for 25 to 30 minutes. Therefore, faculty wishing to incorporate a low-risk strategy might consider dividing the class time into segments with minilectures followed by short exercises involving active learning. This low-risk approach would be especially helpful to the increasing number of faculty who face the challenge of teaching students in three-hour class periods that meet one evening per week. More important, low-risk interactive strategies enable faculty members to develop experience in and have success with new techniques.

TABLE 1

A COMPARISON OF LOW- AND HIGH-RISK ACTIVE LEARNING STRATEGIES

Dimension	Low-Risk Strategies	High-Risk Strategies
Class Time Required	Relatively short	Relatively long
Degree of Structure	More structured	Less structured
Degree of Planning	Meticulously planned	Spontaneous
Subject Matter	Relatively concrete	Relatively abstract
Potential for Controversy	Less controversial	Very controversial
Students' Prior Knowledge of the Subject Matter	Better informed	Less informed
Students' Prior Knowledge of the Teaching Technique	Familiar	Unfamiliar
Instructor's Prior Experience with the Teaching Technique	Considerable	Limited
Pattern of Interaction	Between faculty and students	Among students

In terms of the degree of planning and organization required, more highly structured strategies involve less risk than less structured ones. Highly structured strategies described previously include short writing activities, feedback lectures, case studies, exercises in Guided Design, and formal debates. Conversely, responsive lectures, role playing, and small discussion groups typically involve less structure. When employing any of the strategies discussed in this monograph, faculty might incorporate structure to a greater or lesser degree. For example, the skillful use of questioning in class could involve crafting a careful sequence of thought-provoking recitation questions focused on understanding a single concept as opposed to a series of questions that stimulate divergent thinking about moral issues. The degree of structure imposed therefore depends upon the faculty member's preference.

In this same vein, faculty can vary in the degree of spontaneity in the classroom with which they feel comfortable; some routinely write meticulously detailed lecture notes complete with formal definitions, illustrative examples, and humorous remarks, while others prefer to rely upon skeletal notes, a repertoire of possible examples, and the mood of the moment to provide humor. Neither approach is better or worse than the other; clearly, one's best style is more a matter of personal preference than of proper pedagogical practice. The less planned the activity is in advance, however, the greater the risk involved, and few things are riskier for most faculty than anticipating that a brilliant strategy promoting active learning will emerge from one's unconscious like a bolt of lightening five minutes before class begins.

Another dimension that can influence the level of risk associated with a particular strategy involves the specific subject of the lesson. When the subject is relatively concrete, the class session is less likely to encounter difficulties than when the subject is relatively abstract. For example, exercises in active learning based upon short, specific reading assignments completed during class time involve less risk, for both instructors and students, than exercises based on the vagaries of "what you learned in high school." Another related factor involves the subject's potential for controversy; the lower the level of controversy and volatility associated with the topic, the less risk involved. When the subject is highly controversial because it involves matters of personal values, challenges deeply held beliefs, or identifies personal prejudices, the potential for discussions to become excessively heated and difficult to keep focused increases; at the other extreme, however, a discussion about a totally noncontroversial issue merely runs the risk of becoming boring.

Students' knowledge of the subject will also influence the risk involved in an activity; the better informed the students, the lower the risk of the instructor's disappointment. Several simple yet effective approaches could be helpful. An assessment of the extent of students' knowledge about the subject before beginning an activity can help reduce risk. The results of such an assessment will allow faculty to plan materials or strategies designed to enable students to learn appropriate material: study guides, short writing assignments, or assigned readings. Perhaps the safest approach of all is to provide a

. . . clearly, one's best style is more a matter of personal preference than of proper pedagogical practice.

short in-class reading assignment that will give students a common base of knowledge.

Prior exposure to any given teaching technique also influences the level of risk for both students and instructors; the less experience that either students or instructors have, the greater the risk. This observation suggests that strategies promoting active learning attempted early in the semester, when students are unfamiliar with a faculty member's particular style of teaching and uncertain about his or her personal trustworthiness, will involve greater levels of risk than those same activities attempted later in the semester. A related issue is how well students like a particular strategy. Students need to be forced to learn the art of discussion (and other interactive techniques) (Gregory 1984). Previously cited research suggests that students' level of motivation will become higher once they are familiar with a given strategy. Similarly, until an instructor becomes comfortable with his or her students and is practiced in a particular approach, he or she will be faced with a high-risk situation as well.

The use of strategies promoting active learning dramatically changes the pattern of communication observed in the classroom. The greater the emphasis placed on interaction only between faculty and students, the less the risk; the more an instructor encourages dialogue between students, the greater the risk. In small groups, students might not be skilled listeners or might lack experience as leaders and thus divert from the task. Shy students might not participate in conversations with other students. Faculty can anticipate that such problems will diminish with planning and practice.

As used throughout this monograph, strategies for active learning involve students in doing things and thinking about the things they are doing. It is important to remember that faculty members still exercise considerable control over what does and does not happen in the classroom. The degree to which faculty control the dimensions of time, material, and structure, and the technique chosen delimits the operational level of risk. Thus, the process of selecting that evaluates and weaves each dimension into its final form determines the probability of its success for any given faculty member.

Further, instructional approaches can be usefully classified in terms of the level of students' activity they promote and the level of risk they entail. Table 2 classifies the previously discussed teaching techniques in terms of these two criteria.

TABLE 2

A CLASSIFICATION OF INSTRUCTIONAL STRATEGIES ACCORDING TO STUDENTS' ACTIVITY AND RISK INVOLVED

Students Are Active/Lower Level of Risk	Students Are Active/Higher Level of Risk
Structured small-group discussion	Role playing
Surveys or questionnaires	Small-group presentations
Demonstrations	Presentations by individual students
Self-assessment activities	Guided imagery exercise
Brainstorming activities	Unstructured small-group discussion
In-class writing	Responsive lecture
Field trips	
Library tours	
Quizzes or examinations	
Lecture with pauses	
Lecture with discussion	
Feedback lecture	
Guided lecture procedure	
Students Are Inactive/Lower Level of Risk	**Students Are Inactive/Higher Level of Risk**
Show a film for the entire class period	Invite a guest lecturer of unknown quality
Lecture for the entire period	

Faculty can successfully overcome each of the major obstacles or barriers to the use of active learning and reduce the possibility of failure by gradually incorporating teaching strategies involving more activity from students and greater risks into their regular teaching style. Before this process can take place, however, faculty should first identify those strategies that they currently use and with which they are comfortable. Then, based on their knowledge of other strategies, they can determine which new techniques would be suitable for implementing on a trial basis during the next semester. To help this process, a self-assessment instrument as shown in table 3 is suggested. Note that the strategies are listed in an approximate ascending order of risk.

After filling out the survey, faculty are advised to examine the "Next Time" column and then select the strategy with the least risk for study and implementation. (The list of references at the end of this monograph provides sufficient resources to allow a faculty member to read and evaluate the promises and problems associated with any given technique.) If the strategy selected still seems suitable, the next step is to initiate a careful planning process using the other key dimensions

TABLE 3

A SURVEY OF CLASSROOM TEACHING METHODS

Directions: Faculty use class time in many different ways. Describe the teaching strategies you have used during a semester in the class you teach most often. First, carefully read the list of teaching strategies and indicate with a check mark if you used this teaching method the *last time* you taught this class. Then indicate with a check mark whether you would be willing to try this teaching method the *next time* you teach this class.

Teaching Strategy	Last Time	Next Time
I lectured the whole period.	☐	☐
I showed a film or video the entire period.	☐	☐
I used demonstrations during lecture.	☐	☐
I gave a "surprise" short quiz (graded or ungraded).	☐	☐
I lectured, using pauses.	☐	☐
I assigned a short writing activity without having class discussion afterward.	☐	☐
I had students complete a self-assessment activity (e.g., complete a questionnaire about their beliefs, values, attitudes).	☐	☐
I had students complete a survey instrument.	☐	☐
I used the feedback lecture.	☐	☐
I used the guided lecture procedure.	☐	☐
I lectured with at least 15 minutes of time devoted to class discussion.	☐	☐
I assigned a short writing activity that was followed by at least 15 minutes of class discussion.	☐	☐
I led a class discussion about an audiovisual stimulus (e.g., a picture, cartoon, graph, song) lasting 15 minutes or more.	☐	☐
I assigned an in-class reading activity that was followed by a significant class discussion lasting 15 minutes or more.	☐	☐
I had students engage in a problem-solving game or simulation.	☐	☐
I had students engage in a brainstorming activity.	☐	☐
I assigned a small-group discussion or project focused on structured questions.	☐	☐
I assigned a student-centered class discussion (i.e., students developed the questions and led the discussion that followed).	☐	☐
I assigned presentations to individual students (e.g., speeches, reports).	☐	☐
I assigned small-group presentations (e.g., debates, panel discussions).	☐	☐
I had students engage in a role-playing activity.	☐	☐
I used a responsive lecture.	☐	☐

associated with risk: time, material, and structure. The beginner, regardless of selected technique, should devise a short activity based on carefully structured material provided in the classroom (lecture, handout, audiovisual stimulus, and so on). As confidence develops, constraints on planning can be successfully loosened.

It must be acknowledged that some strategies promoting active learning are more easily implemented in particular disciplines than in others. For example, role playing might be a more appropriate activity in literature, psychology, or nursing classes than in math or chemistry courses. Group work, brainstorming, debates, and writing, however, have been used productively in various science courses. In short, while not every technique described earlier is equally appropriate for every academic discipline, no discipline can categorically disavow *all* strategies promoting active learning. Further, sound educational practice should never be summarily dismissed simply because it is difficult to implement.

The Role of Faculty Developers

Workshops on methods and techniques of instruction are one of the most common forms of faculty development on college and university campuses (Erickson 1986). In light of all that has been said thus far, it seems reasonable to recommend that faculty developers or faculty development committees plan and implement frequent programs on the use of active learning in the classroom. In addition to the short and general consciousness-raising sessions, detailed workshops on building skills should be offered.

Faculty developers should recognize and address several characteristics that influence the adoption of innovation in their programs (Rogers 1983, pp. 15–16):

1. *Relative advantage,* the degree to which an innovation is perceived as better than the idea it supersedes;
2. *Compatibility,* the degree to which an innovation is perceived as being consistent with existing values, past experiences, and needs of potential adopters;
3. *Complexity,* the degree to which an innovation is perceived as difficult to understand and use;
4. *Trialability,* the degree to which an innovation could be experimented with on a limited basis; and
5. *Observability,* the degree to which the results of an innovation are visible to others.

Successful programs for enhancing teaching should be guided by these principles and should let faculty know that active learning does have advantages over lecturing and that low-risk, simple strategies (such as keeping silent for three two-minute periods or having periodic writing exercises) can gradually be incorporated into existing teaching styles without being disruptive. Toward this end, the use of strategies promoting active learning should become a frequently discussed issue in campus-based faculty development newsletters and publications. It is not enough, however, simply to send faculty handouts on how to do it, for adopting new strategies at higher levels of risk can make even hardened, experienced teachers feel very vulnerable. They need follow-up and personal support, either from the development office or from a network of colleagues that has been created for that purpose.

> As the flow of blood is essential to human life, so direct personal contact is essential to the propagation of innovation. . . . Direct personal contacts are the medium through which innovations must flow. Innovation diffusion is directly proportional to the number, frequency, depth, and duration of such contact (House 1974, p. 11).

In addition to sponsoring programs in which strategies promoting active learning are the workshop's content, workshop leaders should skillfully model the process of active learning in all faculty development programs. In innumerable professional sessions, presenters have lectured on how to lead a discussion or tediously described the elements that comprise an exciting classroom. Not all topics are suitable for modeling interactive strategies, but professional development programs on teaching techniques certainly are! Preconceptions, however, are difficult to overcome. Recently, a keynote speaker was asked to give a presentation on critical thinking techniques to senior administrators at a national convention. When he shared his plans for an interactive and experiential session where participants would evaluate the pros and cons of implementing critical thinking in the classroom, the organizer hesitated over the choice of instructional strategies and finally blurted out, "After all, these *are* college presidents!" To the coordinator's great relief, even college presidents appreciated an interactive session and the program was enthusiastically received. (See Eison, Janzow, and Bonwell 1990 for more than 20 specific suggestions to help workshop facilitators ensure success in these efforts.)

Faculty developers might also introduce the concept of active learning into campuswide discussions of curricular reform. A national survey of current campus trends notes that more than nine out of 10 colleges and universities had recently completed or were in the midst of revising the curriculum (El-Khawas 1988). Especially common topics were placing greater emphasis on improving students' writing skills, creating new general education requirements, and putting greater emphasis on the freshman year. One proposal for increasing the use of strategies promoting active learning across the campus would be to ensure that when proposals for new or revised courses or college curricula are discussed, committees not only consider *what* will be taught but also give full and equal weight to *how* it will be taught.

The Role of Campus Administrators

One important arena in which campus administrators can help set the stage for greater use of active learning is through the recognition and reward of excellent teaching in general and the adoption of innovations in the classroom in particular. Unfortunately, these goals are often not emphasized; while paying lip service to "teaching excellence," most institutions have other agendas, even though the faculty's goals might differ. A major study found that a significant number of faculty place a high priority on teaching. Thirty-five to 45 percent of the faculty expressed these sentiments in research universities, 55 to 75 percent of the faculty in doctorate-granting institutions, 75 percent of those in comprehensive institutions, and 75 to 90 percent of faculty in liberal arts colleges. Of particular interest is that even in the research institutions, only 15 percent of the faculty reported being heavily committed to research (Clark 1987, p. 86). Thus, although the professoriat nationwide appears to be strongly committed to teaching, the system does little to reward or nurture that interest.

In what ways might administrators address this disparity? A recent and especially useful text suggests that senior academic officials must create a climate for improving instruction by changing the social and cultural mores defining the role of teaching at any institution (Weimer 1990). Specifically, they include:

- *Establish the same climate of inquiry about the art of teaching applied to research in other academic areas.* Scholarship about teaching should be encouraged, valued, and discussed.
- *Provide instructors with clear and consistent communications about expectations regarding teaching.* Faculty become frustrated and confused when they are told that teaching plays a vital institutional role but note that rewards are primarily for research.
- *Encourage alternative instructional strategies to meet the needs of students' different learning styles.* Students are inherently different, and their diversity enhances different styles of teaching.
- *Create a nurturing atmosphere that supports risk.* Faculty must feel that it is all right to try a new strategy, even if first attempts are less than satisfactory.

Many institutions have superficially attempted to meet these objectives by relying almost exclusively on teaching awards. This singular approach seldom works, however.

> *At present, the universities are as uncongenial to teaching as the Mojave Desert is to a clutch of Druid priests. If you want to restore a Druid priesthood, you cannot do it by offering prizes for Druid-of-the-Year. If you want Druids, you must grow forests* (Arrowsmith, cited in Weimer 1990, p. 134).

Broader initiatives are needed to infuse a commitment to teaching throughout an institution.

A comprehensive program that administrators can implement to demonstrate their commitment to creating an environment supportive of teaching (Cochran 1989) would include:

- *Employment policies and practices*
  1. As an integral part of the hiring process, assess a prospective faculty member's teaching effectiveness and potential to be effective.
  2. Ensure that students regularly evaluate classroom instruction.

3. Require regular observation by peers as a key component in promoting and granting tenure to faculty.
4. "Set aside the singular approach of evaluating research and publications, and develop alternative means of demonstrating faculty intellectual vitality . . ." (Cochran 1989, p. 58). Inevitably, some readers will now be pondering the question, "Aren't effective teaching and productivity in research related?" Though a detailed analysis of this question goes well beyond the scope of this monograph, considerable empirical research has addressed this question, and the results clearly indicate that the two are essentially unrelated (Centra 1983; Feldman 1987).

- *Instructional development activities*
  1. Create an organized unit or program charged with enhancing teaching.
  2. Provide ongoing workshops to enhance teaching for faculty, teaching assistants, and part-time personnel.
  3. Make funds available to support innovative changes in curriculum or alternative teaching strategies.
- *Strategic administrative actions*
  1. Ensure that the physical plant encourages a positive teaching and learning environment.
  2. Promote research designed to improve the quality of instruction.
  3. Collect institutional data on the effectiveness of teaching and use it as a means of improving instruction.
  4. Establish college-based teaching enhancement committees to allocate funds for appropriate projects.
  5. Consistently reinforce the importance of effective teaching through news releases, position papers, and public presentations focusing attention on exciting and innovative classroom activities.

A legitimate concern associated with this proposed program is the financial cost. Although some of the suggestions, such as creating a center for teaching and learning or improving the physical plant, could incur high costs, in reality most of the activities Cochran lists can be accomplished with minimal institutional resources. A $200 grant to an instructor for buying materials to assist with an innovative classroom project reaps large dividends in terms of the attitude of institutional support it portrays to faculty. The real key to establishing a supportive environment for innovative teaching is to create administrative mechanisms that consistently promote, reward, and publicize excellence in the classroom.

The Role of Educational Researchers

Those familiar with the literature would agree that the "entire field of research on college teaching is underdeveloped" (Green and Stark 1986, p. 19). Certainly this generalization holds true for research on active learning, and what had been done has serious limitations. To cite but one example, most published articles on active learning in professional journals of higher education lack either a theoretical framework or a scientific foundation, and it is "the scientific method, more than any other procedure known to man, [that] provides the basis for intelligent change: change based on systematic knowledge rather than on improvisation, hunch, or dogma (Sanford 1965, p. v). Unfortunately, although more than 25 years have passed since that statement was made, the current body of literature fails to meet this most basic criterion. Most articles the authors have located have been primarily descriptive pieces rather than empirical investigations. Although how-to articles are often useful in generating new insights and ideas among faculty, more rigorous studies must be undertaken to provide a scientific foundation for future practice.

A great need also exists for more current research. Many studies are out of date, either chronologically or methodologically. For instance, perhaps the most extensive review and analysis of research focused on the lecture was conducted in the late 1960s (Verner and Dickinson 1967). Since that time, with the exception of several studies exploring taking notes, little research on lecture methods has been undertaken (McKeachie et al. 1986). Because the lecture has served as the basis by which many other teaching methods have been evaluated, an extensive body of literature is available comparing the relative efficacy of the lecture method with other strategies, but much of this literature is now dated as well. The often-cited box-score analysis of the effectiveness of lectures versus discussion (McKeachie et al. 1986) includes studies ranging in publication dates from 1928 to 1964. At a minimum, these studies now need to be replicated, given the multitude of significant changes in the characteristics of today's undergraduates compared to those who attended college 20 to 30 years ago. As every national report has reminded us, the entry skills of today's freshmen have been steadily declining: 30 to 40 percent lack basic competency in computation, reading, and writing. These differences alone will have a powerful effect on students' responses to teaching methods.

Not only have students changed but so also have the research methods used to evaluate the effectiveness of teaching strategies. The method of meta-analysis used so effectively in the late 1980s was not proposed until 1976 (Cohen, Ebeling, and Kulik 1981). Essentially, this method employs a more sophisticated approach to statistically synthesizing the effects of several studies. Researchers locate appropriate studies on an issue through the use of defined and replicable criteria, use quantitative techniques to describe the studies' features and outcomes, and statistically summarize the results and explore salient relationships. This approach can lead to different, presumably more precise, results. For instance, a 1979 analysis of 18 studies on questioning strategies in the classroom concluded that "whether teachers use predominantly higher cognitive questions or predominantly fact questions makes little difference in student[s'] achievement" (Philip Winne, cited in Pollio 1989, p. 15). A meta-analysis in 1981 using many of these same studies, however, concluded that higher-order questions *did* lead to greater achievement among students.

Other important conceptual issues must also be raised as one reviews past research. Why is the measure of students' achievement defined primarily, if not solely, by students' performance on classroom tests? This issue is especially important, as most classroom examinations have focused on memorizing factual information rather than on questions involving higher-order thinking or an evaluation of students' skills, such as problem solving, writing, or communication. Similarly, one must ask why the lecture method is considered the benchmark for performance. When lecture classes are compared to active learning classes and statistical analyses are performed on group means, the powerful impact of such important characteristics of students as academic ability and preferred learning styles is overlooked.

These and other issues suggest that a clear need exists for scholars of higher education to establish an expanded research agenda.

Similarly, one must ask why the lecture method is considered the benchmark for performance.

• *More research should be focused on modifying the lecture.*

Because the lecture is the most widely used instructional technique, it should be the focus of extensive research to find potentially valuable—and low-risk—modifications to active learning suitable for faculty who prefer not to make dramatic changes in their teaching styles. As reported earlier, learning could be statistically increased if professors would simply remain silent for three two-minute periods during a lecture (Ruhl, Hughes, and Schloss 1987), a change requiring little effort. Ways to improve the presentation of lectures should be more closely examined, and further empirical research is necessary.

• *More studies need to be conducted on alternatives to lectures involving active learning.*

This review has identified a number of large and often surprising gaps in the research literature. More rigorous studies must be undertaken in such areas as discussion, questioning, writing in class, Guided Design, case studies, drama, debate, role plays, and games and simulations. Although some of these techniques have been implemented in large-scale programs around the country, the quantitative evidence to support or reject their adoption is lacking.

• *Researchers must focus on more variables.*

In future research, investigators should use students' level of academic ability and preferences for learning style as independent variables in the design of their research. The finding that field-dependent students, in contrast to field-independent learners, profited significantly more from computer-assisted instruction (MacGregor, Shapiro, and Niemiec 1988) has powerful implications for further research and for the classroom. The often-cited recommendation to use a variety of instructional techniques in the classroom, hoping that all students' learning styles might thus be accommodated, also needs to be tested empirically.

Similarly, the long-term impact of different instructional techniques must be consistently evaluated. Most studies have examined students' performance on tests during a single term or semester. Future research on students' learning in the classroom should also pay attention to the assessment of long-term educational impact, that is, one month, six months, or even one year after the course has been completed. Though logistically difficult to conduct, this type of research will provide the most telling story about the effect that instructors and instructional methods have upon students.

- *Faculty must assume a greater role in educational research.*

The research most likely to improve teaching and learning is that conducted by teachers on questions that they themselves have formulated in response to problems or issues in their own teaching (Cross and Angelo 1988, p. 2).

A caveat must be added, however. Because users of strategies promoting active learning are more likely to be dedicated classroom instructors than they are sophisticated educational researchers, they will need help and support. As previously noted, many of the published reports found in this literature review include relatively simplistic surveys and research methods. The authors hope that in the future such classroom instructors would become co-investigators with individuals more familiar with research design and statistical analysis. Operationally, this matching process could be enhanced by faculty developers or administrative personnel who have a broader perspective of faculty members' talents and interests campuswide.

- *Results of the research should be widely published.*

Finally, the important implications for the classroom of active learning transcends traditional disciplinary boundaries. Investigators should report their results in publications with multidisciplinary readerships, such as *College Teaching, The Journal of Higher Education,* and *Research in Higher Education,* as well as discipline-specific journals, such as *The Teaching of Psychology.*

Simply publishing the results of educational research, however, is not enough. Few would argue with the assertion that "hardly anyone in higher education pays attention to the research and scholarship about higher education" (Keller 1985, p. 7). Regrettably, when compared to other professions like business, medicine, law, dentistry, and public health, teaching is least affected by the findings of professional research (Bolster 1983). Given the increasing public demands for accountability and legislative mandates for assessment, however, it is imperative that the academic community address these concerns.

Such a transformation will not be easy, for people have always resisted change. Over 200 years ago, Benjamin Franklin observed:

> *To get the bad customs of a country changed and new ones, though better, introduced, it is necessary to first remove the prejudices of the people, enlighten their ignorance, and convince them that their interests will be promoted by the proposed changes; and this is not the work of a day* (cited in Rogers 1983, p. 1).

Nor will it be the work of a year. But if faculty, faculty developers, administrators, and educational researchers join in a coordinated and consistent effort to understand and implement active learning in the classroom, an educational revolution *will* occur in the next decade.

REFERENCES

The Educational Resources Information Center (ERIC) Clearinghouse
on Higher Education abstracts and indexes the current literature on
higher education for inclusion in ERIC's data base and announce-
ment in ERIC's monthly bibliographic journal, *Resources in Education* (RIE). Most of these publications are available through the
ERIC Document Reproduction Service (EDRS). For publications cited
in this bibliography that are available from EDRS, ordering number
and price code are included. Readers who wish to order a publication should write to the ERIC Document Reproduction Service,
7420 Fullerton Rd., Suite 110, Springfield VA 22153-2852. (Phone
orders with VISA or MasterCard are taken at 800-443-ERIC or
703-440-1400.) When ordering, please specify the document (ED)
number. Documents are available as noted in microfiche (MF) and
paper copy (PC). If you have the price code ready when you call
EDRS, an exact price can be quoted. The last page of the latest issue
of *Resources in Education* also has the current cost, listed by code.

Adams, James L. 1974. *Conceptual Blockbusting.* Stanford, Cal.: Stanford Alumni Association.

Alibert, Daniel. June 1988. "Towards New Customs in the Classroom."
For the Learning of Mathematics 8: 31–43.

Ambron, Joanna. February 1987. "Writing to Improve Learning in
Biology." *Journal of College Science Teaching* 16: 263–66.

Andrews, John D.W. 1980. "The Verbal Structure of Teacher Questions: Its Impact on Class Discussion." *POD Quarterly* 2(3&4):
129–63.

Association of American Colleges. 1985. *Integrity in the College Curriculum: A Report to the Academic Community.* Project on Rede-
fining the Meaning and Purpose of Baccalaureate Degrees. Washington, D.C.: Author. ED 251 059. 62 pp. MF–01; PC not available
EDRS.

———, Task Group on General Education. 1988. *A New Vitality in
General Education.* Washington, D.C.: Author. ED 290 387. 64 pp.
MF–01; PC not available EDRS.

Astin, Alexander W. 1985. *Achieving Educational Excellence.* San Francisco: Jossey-Bass.

Bailey, Raymond C., and Noel C. Eggleston. Fall 1987. "Active Learning and the Survey Class: Affirmative Action as a Role-Playing Scenario." *Teaching History* 12: 3–9.

Baldridge, J. Victor. March/April 1980. "Managerial Innovation: Rules
for Successful Implementation." *Journal of Higher Education* 51:
117–34.

Bedient, Douglas, George S. Garoian, and Duwayne C. Englert.
Summer 1984. "Self-Instructional Materials for Underprepared
Science Students." *Improving College and University Teaching* 32:
128–34.

Belenky, M.B., B.M. Clinchy, N.R. Goldberger, and J.M. Tarule. 1986.

Women's Ways of Knowing. New York: Basic Books.

Blackburn, Robert T., G. Pellino, A. Boberg, and C. O'Connell. 1980. "Are Instructional Improvement Programs Off-Target?" *1980 Current Issues in Higher Education* 1: 32–48.

Bligh, Donald A. 1972. *What's the Use of Lectures?* Baltimore: Penguin Books.

———, ed. 1986. *Teach Thinking by Discussion.* Guildford, Surrey, Great Britain: Society for Research into Higher Education and NFER-NELSON.

Bloom, B., M. Englehart, E. Furst, W. Hill, and D. Krathwohl, eds. 1956. *Taxonomy of Educational Objectives (Cognitive Domain).* New York: David McKay Co.

Bolster, Arthur S., Jr. August 1983. "Toward a More Effective Model of Research on Teaching." *Harvard Educational Review* 53: 294–308.

Boyer, Ernest L. 1987. *The Undergraduate Experience in America.* New York: Harper & Row.

Brooks, Charles I. April 1985. "A Role-Playing Exercise for the History of Psychology Course." *Teaching of Psychology* 12: 84–85.

Centra, John A. 1983. "Research Productivity and Teaching Effectiveness." *Research in Higher Education* 18(2): 379–89.

Chickering, Arthur W., and Zelda F. Gamson. March 1987. "Seven Principles for Good Practice." *AAHE Bulletin* 39: 3–7. ED 282 491. 6 pp. MF–01; PC–01.

Chism, Nancy, Christopher Jones, Barbara Macce, and Roxanne Mountford. 1989. *Teaching at The Ohio State University: A Handbook.* Columbus: Ohio State Univ., Center for Teaching Excellence.

Christensen, Roland C., and Abby J. Hansen. 1987. *Teaching and the Case Method.* Boston: Harvard Business School.

Clark, Burton R. 1987. *The Academic Life: Small Worlds, Different Worlds.* Princeton, N.J.: Carnegie Foundation for the Advancement of Teaching. ED 299 902. 376 pp. MF–01; PC not available EDRS.

Clark, Richard E. Winter 1983. "Reconsidering Research on Learning from Media." *Review of Educational Research* 53: 445–59.

Claxton, Charles S., and Patricia H. Murrell. 1987. *Learning Styles: Implications for Improving Educational Practices.* ASHE-ERIC Higher Education Report No. 4. Washington, D.C.: Association for the Study of Higher Education. ED 293 478. 116 pp. MF–01; PC–05.

Cloke, Paul. 1987. "Applied Rural Geography and Planning: A Simple Gaming Technique." *Journal of Geography in Higher Education* 11(1): 35–45.

Cochran, Leslie H. 1989. *Administrative Commitment to Teaching.* Cape Girardeau, Mo.: Step Up, Inc.

Cohen, Elizabeth G. 1986. *Designing Groupwork.* New York & London: Columbia Univ., Teachers College.

Cohen, Peter A., Barbara J. Ebeling, and James A. Kulik. 1981. "A Meta-analysis of Outcome Studies of Visual-Based Instruction." *Educational Communication and Technology Journal* 29(1): 26–36.

Cohen, Peter A., James A. Kulik, and Chen-Lin C. Kulik. Summer 1982. "Educational Outcomes of Tutoring: A Meta-analysis of Findings." *American Educational Research Journal* 19: 237–48.

Combs, Arthur W. 1979. *Myths in Education: Beliefs That Hinder Progress and Their Alternatives.* Boston: Allyn & Bacon.

Combs, Howard W., and Graham Bourne. June 1989. "The Impact of Marketing Debates on Oral Communication Skills." *The Bulletin* 52: 21–25.

Cooper, Jim. May 1990. "Cooperative Learning and College Teaching: Tips from the Trenches." *The Teaching Professor* 4: 1–2.

Coscarelli, William C., and Gregory P. White. Summer 1982. "Applying the ID Process to the Guided Design Teaching Strategy." *Journal of Instructional Development* 5: 2–6.

———. 1986. *The Guided Design Guidebook: Patterns in Implementation.* Morgantown, W.V.: National Center for Guided Design.

Costin, Frank. January 1972. "Lecturing versus Other Methods of Teaching: A Review of Research." *British Journal of Educational Technology* 3: 4–30.

Cowan, John. December 1984. "The Responsive Lecture: A Means of Supplementing Resource-Based Instruction." *Educational Technology* 24: 18–21.

Cox, R. June 1967. "Resistance to Change in Examining." *Universities Quarterly* 21: 352–58.

Creed, Thomas. Winter 1986. "Why We Lecture." *Symposium: A Saint John's Faculty Journal* 5: 17–32.

Cross, K. Patricia. 1977. "Not Can, but Will College Teaching Be Improved?" In *Renewing and Evaluating Teaching,* edited by John A. Centra. New Directions for Higher Education No. 17. San Francisco: Jossey-Bass.

———. April 1987. "Teaching for Learning." *AAHE Bulletin* 39: 3–7. ED 283 446. 6 pp. MF–01; PC–01.

———. June 1988. "In Search of Zippers." *AAHE Bulletin* 40: 3–7. ED 299 895. 6 pp. MF–01; PC–01.

———. Fall 1989. "Reforming Undergraduate Education One Class at a Time." *Teaching Excellence: Toward the Best in the Academy.* Honolulu: Professional and Organizational Development in Higher Education.

Cross, K. Patricia., and Thomas A. Angelo. 1988. *Classroom Assessment Techniques: A Handbook for Faculty.* Ann Arbor, Mich.: National Center for Research to Improve Postsecondary Teaching and Learning. ED 317 097. 166 pp. MF–01; PC–07.

Cuban, Larry. November 1982. "Persistence of the Inevitable: The Teacher-Centered Classroom." *Education and Urban Society* 15: 26–41.

Davies, L.J. Fall 1983. "Teaching University Students How to Learn."

Improving College and University Teaching 31: 160–65.

Davies, Norman F., and Margaret Omberg. April 1986. "Peer Group Teaching and the Composition Class." Revised version of a paper presented at an annual meeting of the International Association of Teachers of English as a Foreign Language. ED 274 159. 17 pp. MF–01; PC–01.

Davison, Joyce G. April 1984. "Real Tears: Using Role Plays and Simulations." *Curriculum Review* 23: 91–94.

Day, Susan. October 1989. "Producing Better Writers in Sociology Classes: A Test of the Writing-across-the-Curriculum Approach." *Teaching Sociology* 17: 458–64.

Dewey, John. 1924. *Democracy and Education*. New York: Macmillan.

———. 1963. *Experience and Education*. New York: Collier Books.

Dillon, James T. November 1984. "Research on Questioning and Discussion." *Educational Leadership* 42: 50–56.

———. 1987. "The Multidisciplinary World of Questioning." In *Questions, Questioning Techniques, and Effective Teaching*, edited by William W. Wilen. Washington, D.C.: National Education Association.

Dougherty, Charles J. January 1981. "Philosophical Role-Playing." *Teaching Philosophy* 4: 39–45.

Dubin, Robert, and Thomas C. Taveggia. 1968. "The Teaching-Learning Paradox: A Comprehensive Analysis of College Teaching Methods." Eugene, Ore.: Center for the Advanced Study of Educational Administration. ED 026 966. 78 pp. MF–01; PC–04.

Duncombe, Sydney, and Michael H. Heikkinen. Winter 1988. "Role-Playing for Different Viewpoints." *College Teaching* 36: 3–5.

Dunkel, Patricia, and Sheryl Davy. 1989. "The Heuristic of Lecture Notetaking: Perceptions of American and International Students Regarding the Value and Practice of Notetaking." *English for Specific Purposes* 8: 33–50.

Eble, Kenneth E. 1976. *The Craft of Teaching*. San Francisco: Jossey-Bass.

———. 1983. *The Aims of College Teaching*. San Francisco: Jossey-Bass.

Eisenberg, Carola. 1987. "The Stresses of Beginning Teaching." *On Teaching and Learning* 2: 17–21.

Eison, James. 1988. *Enhancing Student Study Skills: How College Faculty Can Help*. Cape Girardeau, Mo.: Southeast Missouri State Univ., Center for Teaching and Learning.

———. Winter 1990. "Confidence in the College Classroom: Ten Maxims for New Teachers." *College Teaching* 38: 21–25.

Eison, James, and Charles Bonwell. 1988. "Making Real the Promise of Active Learning." Paper presented at a national conference of the American Association for Higher Education, March 12, Washington, D.C.

Eison, James, Fred Janzow, and Charles Bonwell. Summer 1990. "Active Learning in Faculty Development Workshops: Or, Practicing What We Teach." *Journal of Staff, Program, and Organization Development* 8: 81–99.

Eison, James, and Howard Pollio. May 1989. "LOGO II: Bibliographic and Statistical Update." Mimeographed. Cape Girardeau, Mo.: Southeast Missouri State Univ., Center for Teaching and Learning.

Ekroth, Loren. Winter/Spring 1990. "Why Professors Don't Change." In *Teaching Excellence*. Honolulu: Univ. of Hawaii at Manoa, Center for Teaching Excellence.

El-Khawas, Elaine. September 1988. *Campus Trends, 1988*. Higher Education Panel Reports No. 77. Washington, D.C.: American Council on Education. ED 301 121. 70 pp. MF–01; PC–03.

Ellner, Carolyn L., and Carol P. Barnes. 1983. *Studies of College Teaching*. Lexington, Mass.: D.C. Heath & Co.

Erdle, Stephen, Harry G. Murray, and J. Philippe Rushton. August 1985. "Personality, Classroom Behavior, and Student Ratings of College Teaching Effectiveness: A Path Analysis." *Journal of Educational Psychology* 77: 394–407.

Ericksen, Stanford C. 1984. *The Essence of Good Teaching*. San Francisco: Jossey-Bass.

Erickson, G. 1986. "A Survey of Faculty Development Practices." In *To Improve the Academy,* edited by M. Svinicki. Stillwater, Okla.: Professional and Organizational Development Network in Higher Education and National Council for Staff, Program, and Organizational Development.

Eurich, Alvin C. Winter 1964. "The Commitment to Experiment and Innovate in College Teaching." *Educational Record* 45: 49–55.

Evans, Richard I., and Peter K. Leppmann. 1967. *Resistance to Innovation in Higher Education*. San Francisco: Jossey-Bass.

Feldman, Kenneth A. 1987. "Research Productivity and Scholarly Accomplishments of College Teachers as Related to Their Instructional Effectiveness: A Review and Exploration." *Research in Higher Education* 26(1): 227–98.

Ferrante, Reynolds, John Hayman, Mary Susan Carlson, and Harry Phillips. 1988. *Planning for Microcomputers in Higher Education: Strategies for the Next Generation*. ASHE-ERIC Higher Education Report No. 7. Washington, D.C.: Association for the Study of Higher Education. ED 308 796. 117 pp. MF–01; PC–05.

Fisher, Charles F. 1978. "Being There Vicariously by Case Studies." In *On College Teaching,* edited by Ohmer Milton. San Francisco: Jossey-Bass.

Fisher, Kathleen M. Fall 1979. "Lecturing Is a Personalized System of Instruction—For the Lecturer." *Journal of Instructional Development* 3: 9–15.

Fraas, John W. 1982. "The Use of Seven Simulation Activities in a College Economic Survey Course." Paper presented at the Economics in the Community College Workshop, October, Orlando, Florida. ED 227 028. 28 pp. MF–01; PC–02.

Frederick, Peter J. Spring 1986. "The Lively Lecture—Eight Variations." *College Teaching* 34: 43–50.

———. 1987. "Student Involvement: Active Learning in Large Classes." In *Teaching Large Classes Well,* edited by M.G. Weimer. New Directions for Teaching and Learning No. 32. San Francisco: Jossey-Bass.

Fuhrmann, Barbara Schneider, and Anthony F. Grasha. 1983. *A Practical Handbook for College Teachers.* Boston: Little, Brown & Co.

Gaff, Jerry G. 1975. *Toward Faculty Renewal.* San Francisco: Jossey-Bass.

Gage, N.L. 1963. *Handbook of Research on Teaching.* Chicago: Rand McNally.

Galbraith, John K. 1987. "How I Could Have Done Much Better." *On Teaching and Learning* 2: 1–4.

Gall, Meredith D. December 1970. "The Use of Questions in Teaching." *Review of Educational Research* 40: 707–21.

Gershen, Jay A. February 1983. "Use of Experiential Techniques in Interpersonal Skill Training." *Journal of Dental Education* 47: 72–75.

Gleason, Maryellen. Winter 1986. "Better Communication in Large Courses." *College Teaching* 34: 20–24.

Goldschmid, Barbara, and Marcel L. Goldschmid. 1976. "Peer Teaching in Higher Education: A Review." *Higher Education (Amsterdam)* 5: 9–33.

Goodlad, Sinclair, and Beverly Hirst. 1989. *Peer Tutoring: A Guide to Learning by Teaching.* New York: Nichols Publishing.

Green, Patricia J., and Joan S. Stark. 1986. *Approaches to Research on the Improvement of Postsecondary Teaching and Learning: A Working Paper.* Ann Arbor, Mich.: National Center for Research to Improve Postsecondary Teaching and Learning. ED 287 432. 24 pp. MF–01; PC–01.

Gregory, M.W. 1984. "What Should Introductory Courses Do?" In *Rejuvenating Introductory Courses,* edited by K.I. Spear. New Directions for Teaching and Learning No. 20. San Francisco: Jossey-Bass.

Hayes, John R. 1981. *The Complete Problem Solver.* Philadelphia: Franklin Institute Press.

Herwitz, David R. June 1987. "Teaching Skills in a Business Law Setting: A Course in Business Lawyering." *Journal of Legal Education* 37: 261–75.

Hinkle, S., and A. Hinkle. February 1990. "An Experimental Comparison of the Effects of Focused Freewriting and Other Study Strategies on Lecture Comprehension." *Teaching of Psychology* 17: 31–35.

Hofstadter, Richard, and William Smith. 1961. *American Higher Edu-*

cation: A Documentary History. 2 vol. Chicago: Univ. of Chicago Press.

Hoover, Kenneth H. 1980. *College Teaching Today: A Handbook for Postsecondary Instruction.* Boston: Allyn & Bacon.

House, Ernest R. 1974. *The Politics of Educational Innovation.* Berkeley, Cal.: McCutchan.

Hult, Richard E., Jr., Sharon Cohn, and David Potter. 1984. "Differential Effects of Note Taking Ability and Lecture Encoding Structure on Student Learning." Paper presented at an annual meeting of the Eastern Educational Research Association, February, West Palm Beach, Florida. ED 249 246. 12 pp. MF–01; PC–01.

Hyman, Ronald T. 1980. *Improving Discussion Leadership.* New York: Columbia Univ., Teachers College Press.

Jabker, Eugene H., and Ronald S. Halinski. July/August 1978. "Instructional Development and Faculty Rewards." *Journal of Higher Education* 49: 316–28.

Janes, Joseph, and Diane Hauer. 1987. *Now What? Readings on Surviving (and Even Enjoying) Your First Experience at College Teaching.* Littleton, Mass.: Copley Publishing Group.

Johnson, Eldon C. November 1985. "Role Playing in Business Communications." *Journal of Education for Business* 61: 60–63.

Johnson, Joseph, Jane Spalding, Roger Paden, and Abbie Ziffren. 1989. *Those Who Can: Undergraduate Programs to Prepare Arts and Sciences Majors for Teaching.* Washington, D.C.: Association of American Colleges. ED 316 682. 186 pp. MF–01; PC not available EDRS.

Johnston, Jerome, and Susan Gardner. 1989. *The Electronic Classroom in Higher Education: A Case for Change.* Ann Arbor: Univ. of Michigan, National Center for Research to Improve Postsecondary Teaching and Learning.

Katz, Joseph. 1985. "Teaching Based on Knowledge of Students." In *Teaching as Though Students Mattered,* edited by J. Katz. New Directions in Teaching and Learning No. 21. San Francisco: Jossey-Bass.

Katz, Joseph, and Mildred Henry. 1988. *Turning Professors into Teachers.* New York: American Council on Education/Macmillan.

Keller, George. January/February 1985. "Trees without Fruit: The Problem with Research about Higher Education." *Change* 17: 7–10.

Kelly, Brenda Wright, and Janis Holmes. April 1979. "The Guided Lecture Procedure." *Journal of Reading* 22: 602–4.

Kirkpatrick, Larry D., and Adele S. Pittendrigh. March 1984. "A Writing Teacher in the Physics Classroom." *The Physics Teacher* 22: 159–64.

Kleerx, Jan, ed. 1990. *English Blockbook.* Maastricht, The Netherlands: Dutch State School of Translation and Interpreting.

Kowalski, R. August 1987. "Teaching Less and Learning More? A Personal Experience." *Programmed Learning and Educational Tech-*

nology 24: 174–86.

Kraft, Robert G. Fall 1985. "Group-Inquiry Turns Passive Students Active." *College Teaching* 33: 149–54.

Kulik, Chen-Lin C., and James A. Kulik. Winter/Spring 1986. "Effectiveness of Computer-Based Education in Colleges." *Association for Educational Data Systems Journal* 19: 81–108.

Kulik, James A., and Chen-Lin C. Kulik. 1987. "Computer-Based Instruction: What 200 Evaluations Say." Paper presented at an annual convention of the Association for Educational Communications and Technology, February, Atlanta, Georgia. ED 285 521. 9 pp. MF–01; PC–01.

Lachs, Avraham. 1984. "Role Playing and the Case Method in Business Education." Mimeographed. ED 252 649. 24 pp. MF–01; PC–01.

Lambiotte, Judith G., Donald F. Dansereau, Thomas R. Rocklin, Bennett Fletcher, Velma I. Hythecker, Celia O. Larson, and Angela M. O'Donnell. January 1987. "Cooperative Learning and Test Taking: Transfer of Skills." *Contemporary Educational Psychology* 12: 52–61.

Langer, Judith A., and Arthur N. Applebee. 1987. *How Writing Shapes Thinking.* Urbana, Ill.: National Council of Teachers of English.

Levine, Arthur. 1978. *Handbook on Undergraduate Curriculum.* San Francisco: Jossey-Bass.

Lewis, Karron G., and Paul Woodward. 1984. "What Really Happens in Large University Classes?" Paper presented at an AERA annual conference, April, New Orleans, Louisiana. ED 245 590. 41 pp. MF–01; PC–02.

Lewis, Karron G., Paul Woodward, and James Bell. Winter 1988. "Teaching Business Communication Skills in Large Classes." *Journal of Business Communication* 25: 65–86.

Lindquist, J. May 1974. "Political Linkage: The Academic-Innovation Process." *Journal of Higher Education* 45: 323–43.

Lowman, Joseph. 1984. *Mastering the Techniques of Teaching.* San Francisco: Jossey-Bass.

Ma, James C. Fall 1989. "A Survey of Finance Department Computer Usage in the California State University and Colleges." *Journal of Financial Education* 18: 71–74.

McClain, Anita. Summer 1987. "Improving Lectures." *Journal of Optometric Education* 13: 18–20.

McCleery, William. 1986. *Conversations on the Character of Princeton.* Princeton, N.J.: Princeton Univ. Press.

McCoy, Joan, and Harlan Roedel. Winter 1985. "Drama in the Classroom: Putting Life in Technical Writing." *Technical Writing Teacher* 12: 11–17.

McDaniel, E.A. 1987. "Faculty Collaboration for Better Teaching: Adult Learning Principles Applied to Teaching Improvement." In *To Improve the Academy,* edited by Joanne Kurfiss. Stillwater, Okla.: Professional and Organizational Development Network in Higher Education.

MacGregor, Kim S., Jonathan Z. Shapiro, and Richard Niemiec. 1988. "Effects of a Computer-Augmented Learning Environment on Math Achievement for Students with Differing Cognitive Style." *Journal of Educational Computing Research* 4(4): 453–65.

McKeachie, Wilbert J., Paul R. Pintrich, Yi-Guang Lin, and David A.F. Smith. 1986. *Teaching and Learning in the College Classroom: A Review of the Research Literature.* Ann Arbor: Regents of The Univ. of Michigan. ED 314 999. 124 pp. MF–01; PC–05.

McTighe, Jay. 1985. "Questioning for Quality Thinking." Mimeographed. Baltimore: Maryland State Dept. of Education, Div. of Instruction.

Madigan, Robert, and James Brosamer. February 1990. "Improving the Writing Skills of Students in Introductory Psychology." *Teaching of Psychology* 17: 27–30.

Mahler, Sophia, Lily Neumann, and Pinchas Tamir. Spring 1986. "The Class-Size Effect upon Activity and Cognitive Dimensions of Lessons in Higher Education." *Assessment and Evaluation in Higher Education* 11: 43–59.

Mauksch, Hans O. 1980. "What Are the Obstacles to Improving Quality Teaching?" In *Improving Teaching and Institutional Quality.* Current Issues in Higher Education No. 1. Washington, D.C.: American Association for Higher Education. ED 194 004. 63 pp. MF–01; PC–03.

Menges, Robert J. Spring 1988. "Research on Teaching and Learning: The Relevant and the Redundant." *Review of Higher Education* 11: 259–68.

Menges, Robert J., and William C. Rando. Spring 1989. "What Are Your Assumptions? Improving Instruction by Examining Theories." *College Teaching* 37: 54–60.

Meyer, G. January 1935. "An Experimental Study of the Old and New Types of Examination: Methods of Study." *Journal of Educational Psychology* 26: 30–40.

Michalak, Stanley J., Jr. Spring 1989. "Writing More, Learning Less?" *College Teaching* 37: 43–45.

Milton, Ohmer. 1968. "The State of the Establishment." In *Learning and the Professors,* edited by O. Milton and E.J. Shoben, Jr. Athens: Ohio Univ. Press.

———. 1985. *On College Teaching.* San Francisco: Jossey-Bass.

Milton, Ohmer, and James A. Eison. 1983. *Textbook Tests: Guidelines for Item Writing.* New York: Harper & Row.

Milton, Ohmer, Howard Pollio, and James Eison. 1986. *Making Sense of College Grades.* San Francisco: Jossey-Bass.

Moeller, Thomas G. December 1985. "Using Classroom Debates in Teaching Developmental Psychology." *Teaching of Psychology* 12: 207–9.

Mohr, L.B. March 1969. "Determinants of Innovation in Organizations." *American Political Science Review* 63: 111–26.

Moore, Shirley B. Winter 1977. "Large Classes: A Positive Point of View." *Improving College and University Teaching* 25: 20–21.

Myers, Linda L. Spring 1988. "Teachers as Models of Active Learning." *College Teaching* 36: 43–45.

National Association of Student Personnel Administrators. 1987. *A Perspective on Student Affairs: A Statement Issued on the 50th Anniversary of* The Student Personnel Point of View. Washington, D.C.: Author.

Newell, George E. October 1984. "Learning from Writing in Two Content Areas: A Case Study/Protocol Analysis." *Research in the Teaching of English* 18: 265–87. ED 293 390. 28 pp. MF–01; PC–02.

Ney, James W. 1989. "Teaching English Grammar Using Collaborative Learning in University Courses." Tempe: Arizona State Univ. ED 311 463. 33 pp. MF–01; PC–02.

Okpala, N.P., and C.O. Onocha. 1988. "The Relative Effects of Two Instructional Methods on Students' Perceived Difficulty in Learning Physics Concepts." *Kenya Journal of Education* 4(1): 147–61.

Osterman, Dean. 1984. "Designing an Alternative Teaching Approach (Feedback Lecture) through the Use of Guided Decision-Making." In *Instructional Development: The State of the Art, II,* edited by Ronald K. Bass and Charles R. Dills. Dubuque, Iowa: Kendall/Hunt Publishing Co. ED 298 903. 27 pp. MF–01; PC–02.

Osterman, Dean, Mark Christensen, and Betty Coffey. January 1985. "The Feedback Lecture." IDEA Paper No. 13. Manhattan: Kansas State Univ., Center for Faculty Evaluation & Development.

Paget, Neil. January 1988. "Using Case Methods Effectively." *Journal of Education for Business* 63: 175–80.

Penner, Jon G. 1984. *Why Many College Teachers Cannot Lecture.* Springfield, Ill.: Charles C. Thomas.

Perry, W.G. 1968. *Forms of Intellectual and Ethical Development in the College Years.* New York: Holt, Rhinehart & Winston.

Pollio, Howard R. 1987. "Practical Poetry: Metaphoric Thinking in Science, Art, Literature, and Nearly Everywhere Else." Teaching-Learning Issues No. 60. Knoxville: Univ. of Tennessee, Learning Research Center.

———. 1989. "Any Questions, Please?" Teaching-Learning Issues No. 66. Knoxville: Univ. of Tennessee, Learning Research Center.

Rabinowitz, Fredric E. April 1989. "Creating the Multiple Personality: An Experiential Demonstration for an Undergraduate Abnormal Psychology Class." *Teaching of Psychology* 16: 69–71.

Rau, William, and Barbara Sherman Heyl. April 1990. "Humanizing the College Classroom: Collaborative Learning and Social Organization among Students." *Teaching Sociology* 18: 141–55.

Riechmann, Sheryl Wetter, and Anthony F. Grasha. July 1974. "A Rational Approach to Developing and Assessing the Construct Validity of a Student Learning Style Scales Instrument." *Journal of Psychology* 87: 213–23.

Rogers, Everett M. 1983. *Diffusion of Innovations.* 3d rev. ed. New York: Free Press.

Rogers, Frances A. March/April 1987. "Videotapes as a Learning Tool in Biology." *Journal of College Science Teaching* 16: 458–61.

Romm, Tsilia, and Sophia Mahler. 1986. "A Three-Dimensional Model for Using Case Studies in the Academic Classroom." *Higher Education (Amsterdam)* 15: 677–96.

Romney, Marshall B. Spring 1984. "Teaching Accounting Information Systems Using a Case Study Approach." *Journal of Accounting Education* 2: 145–51.

Rosenshine, Barak. December 1968. "To Explain: A Review of Research." *Educational Leadership* 26: 303–9.

———. August 1970. "Enthusiastic Teaching: A Research Review." *School Review* 78: 499–514.

Rowe, Mary Budd. 1974. "Wait Time and Rewards as Instructional Variables: Their Influence on Language, Logic, and Fate Control." *Journal of Research in Science Teaching* 11(2): 81–94.

———. 1980. "Pausing Principles and Their Effects on Reasoning in Science." In *Teaching the Sciences,* edited by Florence B. Brawer. New Directions for Community Colleges No. 31. San Francisco: Jossey-Bass.

Rudolph, Frederick. 1962. *The American College and University: A History.* New York: Alfred A. Knopf.

Ruhl, Kathy L., Charles A. Hughes, and Patrick J. Schloss. Winter 1987. "Using the Pause Procedure to Enhance Lecture Recall." *Teacher Education and Special Education* 10: 14–18.

Rutherford, William L. 1977. "An Investigation of How Teachers' Concerns Influence Innovation Adoption." Revised version of a paper presented at an annual meeting of the American Educational Research Association, April, New York. ED 251 426. 31 pp. MF–01; PC–02.

Ryan, Michael P., and Gretchen G. Martens. 1989. *Planning a College Course: A Guidebook for the Graduate Teaching Assistant.* Ann Arbor, Mich.: National Center for Research to Improve Postsecondary Teaching and Learning.

Sanford, Nevitt S., ed. 1965. *The American College.* New York: John Wiley & Sons.

Schermer, Joy. Winter 1988. "Visual Media, Attitude Formation, and Attitude Change in Nursing Education." *Educational Communication and Technology Journal* 36: 197–210.

Schomberg, Steven F., ed. 1986. *Strategies for Active Teaching and Learning in University Classrooms.* Minneapolis: Univ. of Minnesota.

Schroeder, Hal, and David G. Ebert. April 1983. "Debates as a Business and Society Teaching Technique." *Journal of Business Education* 58: 266–69.

Shakhashiri, Bassam Z. November 1984. "Lecture Demonstrations."

Journal of Chemical Education 61: 1010–11.

Siegfried, John J., and Rendigs Fels. September 1979. "Research on Teaching College Economics: A Survey." *Journal of Economic Literature* 17: 923–69.

Sistek, Vladimir. 1986. "How Much Do Our Students Learn by Attending Lectures?" Paper presented at an annual conference of the Society for Teaching and Learning in Higher Education, June, Guelph, Ontario. ED 271 079. 10 pp. MF–01; PC–01.

Slavin, Robert E. November 1983. "When Does Cooperative Learning Increase Student Achievement?" *Psychological Bulletin* 94: 429–45.

Smith, Stanley G., Loretta L. Jones, and Michael L. Waugh. Autumn 1986. "Production and Evaluation of Interactive Videodisc Lessons in Laboratory Instruction." *Journal of Computer-Based Instruction* 13: 117–21.

Stark, Joan S., Malcolm A. Lowther, Michael P. Ryan, Sally Smith Bomotti, Michele Genthon, Lynne C. Haven, and Gretchen G. Martens. 1988. *Reflections on Course Planning: Faculty and Students Consider Influences and Goals.* Ann Arbor, Mich.: National Center for Research to Improve Postsecondary Teaching and Learning. ED 316 067. 225 pp. MF–01; PC–09.

Stuart, John, and R.J.D. Rutherford. September 1978. "Medical Student Concentration during Lectures." *Lancet* 2: 514–16.

Study Group on the Conditions of Excellence in American Higher Education. 1984. *Involvement in Learning: Realizing the Potential of American Higher Education.* Washington, D.C.: National Institute of Education/U.S. Dept. of Education. ED 246 833. 127 pp. MF–01; PC–06.

Svinicki, Marilla D., and Nancy M. Dixon. Fall 1987. "The Kolb Model Modified for Classroom Activities." *College Teaching* 35: 141–46.

Sweeney, M. Jane, John J. Siegfried, Jennie E. Raymond, and James T. Wilkinson. Fall 1983. "The Structure of the Introductory Economics Course in United States Colleges." *Journal of Economic Education* 14: 68–75.

Tanis, David O. November 1984. "Why I Do Demonstrations." *Journal of Chemical Education* 61: 1010–11.

Thielens, Wagner, Jr. 1987. "The Disciplines and Undergraduate Lecturing." Paper presented at an annual meeting of the American Educational Research Association, April, Washington, D.C. ED 286 436. 57 pp. MF–01; PC–03.

Tiberius, Richard G. 1990. *Small Group Teaching: A Trouble-Shooting Guide.* Toronto: Ontario Institute for Studies in Education.

Verner, Coolie, and Gary Dickinson. Winter 1967. "The Lecture: An Analysis and Review of Research." *Adult Education* 17: 85–100.

Wales, Charles E. February 1979. "Does How You Teach Make a Difference?" *Engineering Education* 69: 394–98.

Wales, Charles E., and Anne Nardi. November 1982. "Teaching Decision-Making with Guided Design." IDEA Paper No. 9. Manhattan: Kansas State Univ., Center for Faculty Evaluation & Development.

Wales, Charles E., Anne H. Nardi, and Robert A. Stager. 1987. *Thinking Skills: Making a Choice*. Morgantown, W.V.: Center for Guided Design.

Wales, Charles E., and Robert A. Stager. 1978. *The Guided Design Approach*. Englewood Cliffs, N.J.: Educational Technology Publications.

Ward, Thomas J., Jr., and Henry T. Clark III. 1987. "The Effect of Field Dependence and Outline Condition on Learning High- and Low-Structure Information from a Lecture." *Research in Higher Education* 27(3): 259–72.

Watkins, Beverly T. 6 June 1990a. "Colleges Test Case-Study Method to Help Future Teachers Cope with Real-Life Problems They Will Encounter on the Job." *Chronicle of Higher Education* 36: A13+.

———. 18 July 1990b. "More and More Professors in Many Academic Disciplines Routinely Require Students to Do Extensive Writing." *Chronicle of Higher Education* 36: A13+.

Weimer, Maryellen Gleason. February 1989. "Who's Doing All the Work." *Teaching Professor* 3: 1.

———. 1990. *Improving College Teaching*. San Francisco: Jossey-Bass.

———, ed. 1987. *Teaching Large Classes Well*. New Directions for Teaching and Learning No. 32. San Francisco: Jossey-Bass.

Wenk, Virginia A., and Robert J. Menges. March/April 1985. "Using Classroom Questions Appropriately." *Nurse Educator* 10: 19–24.

Wheatley, Jack. April 1986. "The Use of Case Studies in the Science Classroom." *Journal of College Science Teaching* 15: 428–31.

Whiteman, Victor L., and Margaret Nielsen. Fall 1986. "An Experiment to Evaluate Drama as a Method for Teaching Social Work Research." *Journal of Social Work Education* 3: 31–42.

Whitman, Neal A. 1988. *Peer Teaching: To Teach Is to Learn Twice*. ASHE-ERIC Higher Education Report No. 4. Washington, D.C.: Association for the Study of Higher Education. ED 305 016. 103 pp. MF–01; PC–05.

Wilen, William W. 1986. *Questioning Skills for Teachers*. 2d ed. Washington, D.C.: National Education Association. ED 310 098. 35 pp. MF–01; PC not available EDRS.

Williams, Gwendoline. August 1985. "The Case Method: An Approach to Teaching and Learning." In *The Professional Preparation and Development of Educational Administrators in Commonwealth Developing Areas: A Symposium*. ED 276 135. 31 pp. MF–01; PC–02.

Wolfe, Joseph. September 1985. "The Teaching Effectiveness of Games in Collegiate Business Courses: A 1973–1983 Update." *Simulation-and-Games* 16: 251–58.

Wulff, Donald H., Jody D. Nyquist, and Robert D. Abbott. 1987. "Students' Perceptions of Large Classes." In *Teaching Large Classes Well*, edited by M.G. Weimer. New Directions in Teaching and

Learning No. 32. San Francisco: Jossey-Bass.

Young, Art, and Todd Fulwiler, eds. 1986. *Writing across the Disciplines: Research into Practice.* Upper Montclair, N.J.: Boynton/Cook Publishers.

INDEX

A

Active learning, 1, 2
       barriers to use of, 59
       costs, 75
       discomfort with, 57
       faculty resistance, 54–55
       lack of materials, equipment, and funds, 62
       preparation time, 62
       promotion, 3, 33
       risk, 62–64
       role of campus administrators, 73–76
       strategies, 17–19, 33, 66–69
       student resistance, 56
Alternative teaching strategies, 10
Aschner-Gallagher system, 24
Association of American Colleges, 3

B

Brainstorm questions, 26
Business games, 49
Business simulations, 49

C

California State University System, 43
Campus reward systems, 59
Case study method, 38–40
Change in the classroom
      barriers to, 53
      discomfort with, 57
      lack of incentives to , 58
Chemistry laboratory experiments
      on interactive videodiscs, 34
      simulated, 34
Classroom environment, 21
Classroom size, 17
Classroom teaching methods, 70–71
Cognitive Interactive Analysis System, 16
Computer-based instruction, 41–43
Computerization, 43
"Container-dispenser model", 55
Cooperative learning, 43-45
      grades, 44
      group incentives, 44
      individual incentives, 44

D

Debates, 45–46
      in math classes, 46

Democracy and Education, 1
Demonstrations
       student participation, 12
Dewey, John, 1
Discussion strategies, 29–31
Drake University, 34
Drama, 46–47
Dualist learners, 57
Dutch State School of Translation and Interpreting, 34

E

Eastern Michigan State University, 42
Educational researchers
       faculty role as, 79
       focus, 78
       needs, 76
       publications, 79
       role, 76–80
Entry skills of students, 77
Evaluation by tests and quizzes, 11–12

F

Faculty development, 71
       workshops, 71–73
Faculty roles, 54, 65
       self-enchantment, 58
Feedback circle, 56
"Feedback lecture", 13
Focal question, 27
"Forgetting curve", 11
Franklin, Benjamin, 80

G

Games, 47
Great Britain, 30
Guided Design, 40–41, 78
"Guided lecture", 13

H

Harvard Law School, 38, 45
Higher-order thinking, 16

I

Illinois State University, 43
Instructional development activities, 75
Instructional strategies classification, 69
Instructors' goals, 10
Involvement in Learning, 1

K

Key questions, 27

L

Large classes, 14, 61
Learning
       high-risk strategies, 66–69
       low-risk strategies, 66–69
       student involvement, 3
Learning cells, 51
Learning styles, 56
Lecturing, 3, 7
       alternative formats, 13
       effectiveness, 8–10
       length, 9
       pauses, 10
       retention and comprehension, 8–10

M

McGill University, 50, 51
Maryland State Department of Education, 25
Michigan, University of, 41, 42
Mode of instruction, 3
Modified lecture, 7–12
Montana State University, 36

N

National Association of Student Personnel Administrators, 4

O

Open-ended problem solving, 40
Oregon State University, 13
Overcoming barriers to change
       role of faculty, 65

P

Partnerships, 50
Passive learning, 1
Peer counselors, 50
Peer teaching, 50
Peer tutors, 50
Pennsylvania State University, 17
Playground question, 26
Preparation for classes, 61
Professors
       self-definition, 54

Q

Question phrasing, 28
Question types, 24–27
Questioning and discussion, 21

R

Recall of subject matter, 11
"Responsive lecture", 14
Role playing, 47

S

St. John's College, 30
Self-instructional materials, 60
Simulations, 47
Socratic method, 23
Speaking ability, 45
Student-generated questions, 14
Student-instructor rapport, 17
Study Group on the Conditions of Excellence in American Higher
    Education, 4

T

Teacher as dispenser, 55
Teacher evaluation, 21–23
Teaching assistants, 50
Teaching Professor, 54
Techniques of questioning, 27–29
Tests and quizzes, 11
        timing, 11
        evaluative purposes, 12
Texas, University of , 15
        classroom instruction, 15
Traditional teaching practices, 54

V

Value of teaching versus research, 55
Visual-based instruction, 33–35

W

West Virginia University, 40
Westfield State College (New Jersey), 51
Working groups, 50
Writing across the Curriculum, 35
Writing in class, 35–38

ASHE-ERIC HIGHER EDUCATION REPORTS

Since 1983, the Association for the Study of Higher Education (ASHE) and the Educational Resources Information Center (ERIC) Clearinghouse on Higher Education, a sponsored project of the School of Education and Human Development at The George Washington University, have cosponsored the *ASHE-ERIC Higher Education Report* series. The 1991 series is the twentieth overall and the third to be published by the School of Education and Human Development at the George Washington University.

Each monograph is the definitive analysis of a tough higher education problem, based on thorough research of pertinent literature and insitutional experiences. Topics are identified by a national survey. Noted practitioners and scholars are then commissioned to write the reports, with experts providing critical reviews of each manuscript before publication.

Eight monographs (10 before 1985) in the ASHE-ERIC Higher Education Report series are published each year and are available on individual and subscription basis. Subscription to eight issues is $90.00 annually; $70 to members of AAHE, AIR, or AERA; and $60 to ASHE members. All foreign subscribers must include an additional $10 per series year for postage.

To order single copies of existing reports, use the order form on the last page of this book. Regular prices, and special rates available to members of AAHE, AIR, AERA and ASHE, are as follows:

Series	Regular	Members
1990-91	$17.00	$12.75
1988-89	15.00	11.25
1985-87	10.00	7.50
1983-84	7.50	6.00
before 1983	6.50	5.00

Price includes book rate postage within the U.S. For foreign orders, please add $1.00 per book. Fast United Parcel Service available within the contiguous U.S. at $2.50 for each order under $50.00, and calculated at 5% of invoice total for orders $50.00 or above.

All orders under $45.00 must be prepaid. Make check payable to ASHE-ERIC. For Visa or MasterCard, include card number, expiration date and signature. A bulk discount of 10% is available on orders of 15 or more books (not applicable on subscriptions).

Address order to
ASHE-ERIC Higher Education Reports
The George Washington University
1 Dupont Circle, Suite 630
Washington, DC 20036
Or phone (202) 296-2597
Write or call for a complete catalog of ASHE-ERIC Higher Education Reports.

1990 ASHE-ERIC Higher Education Reports

1. The Campus Green: Fund Raising in Higher Education
   Barbara E. Brittingham and Thomas R. Pezzullo

2. The Emeritus Professor: Old Rank - New Meaning
   James E. Mauch, Jack W. Birch, and Jack Matthews

3. "High Risk" Students in Higher Education: Future Trends
   Dionne J. Jones and Betty Collier Watson

4. Budgeting for Higher Education at the State Level: Enigma, Paradox, and Ritual
   Daniel T. Layzell and Jan W. Lyddon

5. Proprietary Schools: Programs, Policies, and Prospects
   John B. Lee and Jamie P. Merisotis

6. College Choice: Understanding Student Enrollment Behavior
   Michael B. Paulsen

7. Pursuing Diversity: Recruiting College Minority Students
   Barbara Astone and Elsa Nuñez-Wormack

8. Social Consciousness and Career Awareness: Emerging Link in Higher Education
   John S. Swift, Jr.

1989 ASHE-ERIC Higher Education Reports

1. Making Sense of Administrative Leadership: The 'L' Word in Higher Education
   Estela M. Bensimon, Anna Neumann, and Robert Birnbaum

2. Affirmative Rhetoric, Negative Action: African-American and Hispanic Faculty at Predominantly White Universities
   Valora Washington and William Harvey

3. Postsecondary Developmental Programs: A Traditional Agenda with New Imperatives
   Louise M. Tomlinson

4. The Old College Try: Balancing Athletics and Academics in Higher Education
   John R. Thelin and Lawrence L. Wiseman

5. The Challenge of Diversity: Involvement or Alienation in the Academy?
   Daryl G. Smith

6. Student Goals for College and Courses: A Missing Link in Assessing and Improving Academic Achievement
   Joan S. Stark, Kathleen M. Shaw, and Malcolm A. Lowther

7. The Student as Commuter: Developing a Comprehensive Institutional Response
   Barbara Jacoby

8. Renewing Civic Capacity: Preparing College Students for Service and Citizenship
   Suzanne W. Morse

1988 ASHE-ERIC Higher Education Reports

1. The Invisible Tapestry: Culture in American Colleges and Universities
   George D. Kuh and Elizabeth J. Whitt

2. Critical Thinking: Theory, Research, Practice, and Possibilities
   Joanne Gainen Kurfiss

3. Developing Academic Programs: The Climate for Innovation
   Daniel T. Seymour

4. Peer Teaching: To Teach is To Learn Twice
   Neal A. Whitman

5. Higher Education and State Governments: Renewed Partnership, Cooperation, or Competition?
   Edward R. Hines

6. Entrepreneurship and Higher Education: Lessons for Colleges, Universities, and Industry
   James S. Fairweather

7. Planning for Microcomputers in Higher Education: Strategies for the Next Generation
   Reynolds Ferrante, John Hayman, Mary Susan Carlson, and Harry Phillips

8. The Challenge for Research in Higher Education: Harmonizing Excellence and Utility
   Alan W. Lindsay and Ruth T. Neumann

1987 ASHE-ERIC Higher Education Reports

1. Incentive Early Retirement Programs for Faculty: Innovative Responses to a Changing Environment
   Jay L. Chronister and Thomas R. Kepple, Jr.

2. Working Effectively with Trustees: Building Cooperative Campus Leadership
   Barbara E. Taylor

3. Formal Recognition of Employer-Sponsored Instruction: Conflict and Collegiality in Postsecondary Education
   Nancy S. Nash and Elizabeth M. Hawthorne

4. Learning Styles: Implications for Improving Educational Practices
   Charles S. Claxton and Patricia H. Murrell

5. Higher Education Leadership: Enhancing Skills through Professional Development Programs
   Sharon A. McDade

6. Higher Education and the Public Trust: Improving Stature in Colleges and Universities
   Richard L. Alfred and Julie Weissman

7. College Student Outcomes Assessment: A Talent Development Perspective
   Maryann Jacobi, Alexander Astin, and Frank Ayala, Jr.

8. Opportunity from Strength: Strategic Planning Clarified with Case Examples
   Robert G. Cope

1986 ASHE-ERIC Higher Education Reports

1. Post-tenure Faculty Evaluation: Threat or Opportunity?
   Christine M. Licata

2. Blue Ribbon Commissions and Higher Education: Changing Academe from the Outside
   Janet R. Johnson and Laurence R. Marcus

3. Responsive Professional Education: Balancing Outcomes and Opportunities
   Joan S. Stark, Malcolm A. Lowther, and Bonnie M.K. Hagerty

4. Increasing Students' Learning: A Faculty Guide to Reducing Stress among Students
   Neal A. Whitman, David C. Spendlove, and Claire H. Clark

5. Student Financial Aid and Women: Equity Dilemma?
   Mary Moran

6. The Master's Degree: Tradition, Diversity, Innovation
   Judith S. Glazer

7. The College, the Constitution, and the Consumer Student: Implications for Policy and Practice
   Robert M. Hendrickson and Annette Gibbs

8. Selecting College and University Personnel: The Quest and the Question
   Richard A. Kaplowitz

1985 ASHE-ERIC Higher Education Reports

1. Flexibility in Academic Staffing: Effective Policies and Practices
   Kenneth P. Mortimer, Marque Bagshaw, and Andrew T. Masland

2. Associations in Action: The Washington, D.C. Higher Education Community
   Harland G. Bloland

3. And on the Seventh Day: Faculty Consulting and Supplemental Income
   Carol M. Boyer and Darrell R. Lewis

4. Faculty Research Performance: Lessons from the Sciences and Social Sciences
   John W. Creswell

5. Academic Program Review: Institutional Approaches, Expectations, and Controversies
   Clifton F. Conrad and Richard F. Wilson

6. Students in Urban Settings: Achieving the Baccalaureate Degree
   Richard C. Richardson, Jr. and Louis W. Bender

7. Serving More Than Students: A Critical Need for College Student Personnel Services
   Peter H. Garland

8. Faculty Participation in Decision Making: Necessity or Luxury?
   Carol E. Floyd

1984 ASHE-ERIC Higher Education Reports

1. Adult Learning: State Policies and Institutional Practices
   K. Patricia Cross and Anne-Marie McCartan

2. Student Stress: Effects and Solutions
   Neal A. Whitman, David C. Spendlove, and Claire H. Clark

3. Part-time Faulty: Higher Education at a Crossroads
   Judith M. Gappa

4. Sex Discrimination Law in Higher Education: The Lessons of the Past Decade. ED 252 169.*
   J. Ralph Lindgren, Patti T. Ota, Perry A. Zirkel, and Nan Van Gieson

5. Faculty Freedoms and Institutional Accountability: Interactions and Conflicts
   Steven G. Olswang and Barbara A. Lee

6. The High Technology Connection: Academic/Industrial Cooperation for Economic Growth
   Lynn G. Johnson

7. Employee Educational Programs: Implications for Industry and Higher Education. ED 258 501.*
   Suzanne W. Morse

8. Academic Libraries: The Changing Knowledge Centers of Colleges and Universities
   Barbara B. Moran

9. Futures Research and the Strategic Planning Process: Implications for Higher Education
   James L. Morrison, William L. Renfro, and Wayne I. Boucher

10. Faculty Workload: Research, Theory, and Interpretation
    Harold E. Yuker

1983 ASHE-ERIC Higher Education Reports

1. The Path to Excellence: Quality Assurance in Higher Education
   Laurence R. Marcus, Anita O. Leone, and Edward D. Goldberg

2. Faculty Recruitment, Retention, and Fair Employment: Obligations and Opportunities
   John S. Waggaman

3. Meeting the Challenges: Developing Faculty Careers. ED 232 516.*
   Michael C.T. Brooks and Katherine L. German

4. Raising Academic Standards: A Guide to Learning Improvement
   Ruth Talbott Keimig

5. Serving Learners at a Distance: A Guide to Program Practices
   Charles E. Feasley

6. Competence, Admissions, and Articulation: Returning to the Basics in Higher Education
   Jean L. Preer

7. Public Service in Higher Education: Practices and Priorities
   Patricia H. Crosson

8. Academic Employment and Retrenchment: Judicial Review and Administrative Action
   Robert M. Hendrickson and Barbara A. Lee

9. Burnout: The New Academic Disease. ED 242 255.*
   Winifred Albizu Melendez and Rafael M. de Guzmán

10. Academic Workplace: New Demands, Heightened Tensions
    Ann E. Austin and Zelda F. Gamson

*Out-of-print. Available through EDRS. Call 1-800-443-ERIC.